The Cross and the Crown

A Series of Studies on the crucifixion and the resurrection of Christ

By KEN CHANT

2

The Cross and the Crown

A Series of Studies on the crucifixion and the resurrection of Christ

By Dr. Ken Chant

Copyright © 2012 Ken Chant

ISBN 978-1-61529-049-9

Vision Publishing

1672 Main St. E 109

Ramona, CA 92065

1-800-9-VISION

www.booksbyvision.com

All rights reserved worldwide

No part of the book may be reproduced in any manner whatsoever without written permission of the author except in brief quotations embodied in critical articles of reviews.

A NOTE ON GENDER

It is unfortunate that the English language does not contain an adequate generic pronoun (especially in the singular number) that includes without bias both male and female. So *"he, him, his, man, mankind,"* with their plurals, must do the work for both sexes. Accordingly, wherever it is appropriate to do so in the following pages, please include the feminine gender in the masculine, and vice versa.

FOOTNOTES

A work once fully referenced will thereafter be noted either by "ibid" or "op. cit."

TABLE OF CONTENTS

PREFACE: THE NEW AND THE OLD 7

SECTION ONE: THE CROSS 9

   CHAPTER ONE: CONFLICT AND CONQUEST 10

   CHAPTER TWO: SAVED TO THE UTTERMOST! 19

   CHAPTER THREE: THE POWER OF THE CROSS 39

SECTION TWO: THE CROWN 57

   CHAPTER FOUR: ALIVE FROM THE DEAD! 58

   CHAPTER FIVE: WITNESSES OF
   THE RESURRECTION 77

   CHAPTER SIX: THE EMPTY TOMB 97

   CHAPTER SEVEN: AN IMMORTAL SOUL? 119

   CHAPTER EIGHT: OUR GLORIOUS GOAL 141

   CHAPTER NINE: THE POWER OF
   HIS RESURRECTION 163

   CHAPTER TEN: LIVING VICTORIOUSLY 185

ADENDUM: Examples of the "Fairytale Principle" 201

BIBLIOGRAPHY 205

ABBREVIATIONS

Abbreviations commonly used for the books of the Bible are

Genesis	Ge	Habakkuk	Hb
Exodus	Ex	Zephaniah	Zp
Leviticus	Le	Haggai	Hg
Numbers	Nu	Zechariah	Zc
Deuteronomy	De	Malachi	Mal
Joshua	Js		
Judges	Jg		
Ruth	Ru	Matthew	Mt
1 Samuel	1 Sa	Mark	Mk
2 Samuel	2 Sa	Luke	Lu
1 Kings	1 Kg	John	Jn
2 Kings	2 Kg	Acts	Ac
1 Chronicles	1 Ch	Romans	Ro
2 Chronicles	2 Ch	1 Corinthians	1 Co
Ezra	Ezr	2 Corinthians	2 Co
Nehemiah	Ne	Galatians	Ga
Esther	Es	Ephesians	Ep
Job	Jb	Philippians	Ph
Psalm	Ps	Colossians	Cl
Proverbs	Pr	1 Thessalonians	1 Th
Ecclesiastes	Ec	2 Thessalonians	2 Th
Song of Songs	Ca *	1 Timothy	1 Ti
Isaiah	Is	2 Timothy	2 Ti
Jeremiah	Je	Titus	Tit
Lamentations	La	Philemon	Phm
Ezekiel	Ez	Hebrews	He
Daniel	Da	James	Ja
Hosea	Ho	1 Peter	1 Pe
Joel	Jl	2 Peter	2 Pe
Amos	Am	1 John	1 Jn
Obadiah	Ob	2 John	2 Jn
Jonah	Jo	3 John	3 Jn
Micah	Mi	Jude	Ju
Nahum	Na	Revelation	Re

Ca is an abbreviation of *Canticles*, a derivative of the Latin name of the *Song of Solomon*, which is sometimes also called the *Song of Songs*.

PREFACE:

THE NEW AND THE OLD

Having the peculiar benefit of living in a house placed between two tennis courts, Blaise Pascal[1] was able to write -

> *"Let no one maintain that I have said nothing new; my arrangement of the material is new. In a game of tennis we both play with the same ball, but one of us uses it to better advantage. I would as soon it were said that I have used well-worn words. The same thoughts, when differently arranged, form a new body of speech; just as the same words differently arranged express new thoughts."*

I hope that is how you will find these chapters. They traverse familiar ground; yet I pray they may still sparkle with freshness. Not because these pages contain stunning new ideas, but because of the personal colour I have sought to build into each paragraph. To paraphrase Pascal just a little: "I have said nothing new; but my arrangement of the material is new."

This course is a close companion to another VCC series, **Immanuel**. But whereas that series deals with the **person** of Christ, this deals with the **work** of Christ. Especially, with the **historical** work of Christ, and even more particularly with the

---

[1] Blaise Pascal was a mathematician, scientist, and devout Christian, born in France in 1623. He was a "thinker of phenomenal power and insight," and his **Pensees** ("Thoughts") - a collection of notes and fragments gathered by friends after his death - has had an immense influence. The above quotation is from **Fragment #4**, in the translation by John Warrington, published by J. M. Dent & Sons Ltd., London. 1973.

events surrounding his **passion** - that is, the crucifixion and the resurrection.

St. Bernard once said, "That which makes us better makes us worse, if we attribute the merit of it to ourselves." I have no illusions about this course making me any better merely because I am its author; but I **would** be a fool if I allowed it to make me worse, by imagining myself to be the source of any merit it might contain. I have made only a husk. The creator of the true bread is Christ.

SECTION ONE:

THE CROSS

CHAPTER ONE:

CONFLICT AND CONQUEST

There is an ancient and apparently anonymous saying: "**The three most beautiful things in the world are a full-rigged ship, a woman with child, and a full moon**." I am not sure about the superlative beauty of the first and last things; but every devoted husband and father rejoices in the wondrous loveliness of a woman with child. And among all such, there has never been a mother so lovely as Mary. From her womb came the Christ, who is himself called

> *"the Fairest of Ten Thousand ... altogether desirable ... the bright Morning Star" (Ca 5:10,16; Re 22:16).*

The first reference in history to that epochal event is found in God's sentence upon Satan:

> *"I will put enmity between you and the woman, and between your seed and her seed; he shall bruise your head, and you shall bruise his heel" (Ge 3:15).*

That could be called the first and greatest gospel sermon (though it was addressed to the Serpent), for those vibrant words contain the essence of God's great program of redemption. Right at the stricken hour of human failure the mercy of God blazons with a promise of salvation. Here, at the beginning of sin, in the moment of human alliance with evil, the Lord declares unending warfare between man and Satan, and he predicts the coming of Christ, and the final defeat of Satan.

Notice how God promised that the Deliverer would be born of a woman, that he would suffer, but that his triumph would be inevitable.

There indeed was a remarkable sermon!

That first announcement, made by the Lord God to Adam and Eve, in the already decaying Garden-cathedral of Eden, forms the best place to begin a study of the passion of Christ -

(I) THE FIRST GOSPEL SERMON

The Father both warned Satan and promised fallen man that

(A) A CONFLICT WOULD BEGIN

Satan had hoped to have man as his full ally in a rebellion against God. But that evil design was foiled by God's declaration of war between the devil and man: *"I will put enmity between you and the woman, and between your seed and hers."*

Satan is held bound by that eternal decree. Because of it, mankind can never become a partner with Satan and his fallen angels in their rebellion, but must ever remain under pitiless onslaught by the powers of darkness, ever writhing under a burden of sin and sorrow, able to find release only by the saving hand of God.

It is strange but true: every time the devil attacks a man or woman he is displaying his absolute subjection to heaven's command!

The wise purpose of the Lord in declaring unending conflict between the powers of evil and the human race was, at the very beginning, to establish a basis of victory for man.

That basis is to loathe the devil and all his ways.

Men fall when they like and listen to Satan, when they put foolish trust in the blandishments of their most bitter enemy. Satan appears to be an ally; but his one aim is always "to steal, to kill, to destroy" (Jn 10:10). Satan is man's foulest foe, and will never be his friend.

The devil even sought to enlist Jesus into his service, only so he might destroy him; but Christ, hating iniquity and loving righteousness (He 1:9), trounced the Evil One.

Just so, that same Serpent entices us; but like Christ, we must spurn him. An abhorrence of everything to do with Satan and his wicked machinations is the soundest basis upon which to build continuing victory over all the malignant works of darkness.

Satan conquers us when he cunningly causes us to love him (or his works), while all the time he hates us and is striving to do us every possible injury. So let us hate him; let us wage undaunted warfare against all of his works; then we shall easily triumph (Ja 4:7).

So, by decreeing truceless warfare between Satan and man, God intended to make us sick of sin, and by this to bring us to repentance, calling upon him for pardon and freedom.

(B) A CHAMPION WOULD BE SENT

This Champion would be of **"the seed of the woman,"** and in the fullness of time he was born in Bethlehem, and was called **Jesus of Nazareth.** In him men and women were to find a mighty ally, one who would lead them to full triumph over sickness and sin.

Satan mustered all his forces, trying to prevent Christ from being born, and to stop him from fulfilling his mission: thus Mary was compelled to give birth to her son among the disease-ridden squalor of a cattle stall; he barely escaped the relentless hatred of King Herod; his parents had to take him on the long and perilous journey to Egypt.

Later came the temptation in the wilderness - a fierce onslaught of hunger and desire extending through 40 days and nights.

Leaving the desert, he several times had to flee the murderous howling mob; then at the end, despite his own earnest plea, he could not evade the agony of Gethsemane, nor the horror of the Roman iron-laced lash, the mockery of his own people, and, finally, the ignominy and torment of the cross.

Yet despite this frenzy of hatred and violence, **Satan failed**.

A Minor Wound

All of those hurts on top of one another left Christ, in the outcome, with nothing worse than a **"bruised heel"** - which is a graphic way of saying Satan was incapable of dealing a mortal blow to Christ. The devil's most awful weapons were finally helpless to inflict on Christ anything more than a superficial wound!

Whatever greater depths of suffering Christ endured at Calvary were pains that he himself willingly embraced. They were not imposed on him. Satan tried to snatch away the life of Jesus, but he failed miserably. Jesus himself laid his life down, by an act of his own will, and by his own power; it was not taken from him. He declared:

> *"No one can take my life. I lay it down by myself.*
> *And I shall take it up again" (Jn 10:17-18).*

It is important to remember that Jesus did all this as "**the seed of the woman**" - he lived, suffered, and died, as a **man.** He laid aside his equality with God, and came to conquer sin and death as a **man** (Ph 2:6-11). Jesus therefore became the first person in history whom death could not forcibly grasp. By the act of **compelling** death to take hold of him, Jesus nullified its power and removed its sting.

A Glorious Triumph

Furthermore, by deliberately yielding himself to death and then, after three days, shaking himself free of it, Christ brought into brilliant reality **a new concept of God's power**. For centuries the Exodus of Israel from Egypt had been spoken of as the crowning feat of God among men. But in Christ a new standard has been achieved: **the resurrection of Jesus from the dead is now the supreme demonstration of Divine might.**

If, in answer to the faith of his Son, God was able to raise him from the dead, how can there by any limit to what he can do for **us**, if we believe as Jesus did?

No wonder Paul shouted -

> *"How immeasurably great is his power in us who believe! It is according to the working of his great might which he accomplished in Christ when he raised him from the dead!" (Ep 1:18-21).*

So Jesus was born that he might become our Champion by winning a representative victory for us, and then by leading us on to personal triumph over Satan. He did this by gladly yielding his life on our behalf (He 2:14-15). Death was the devil's most powerful, most feared weapon. But Christ tore that weapon right out of the enemy's hand - like Benaiah, who slew an Egyptian with his own spear (2 Sa 23:21), so Jesus took hold of the cross, that instrument of death, and by it annihilated Satan's power of death.

Jesus has now become the conquering Captain of our salvation; and as we link ourselves with him in this triumph, we have his promise that he will lead us irresistibly home to eternal glory!

(C) A CONQUEST WOULD BE GAINED

While the Serpent could do no more than bruise Jesus' "heel", it was said of the Lord, **"He shall bruise (Satan's) head!"**

The contrast is between a superficial wound and a mortal one.

The idea is that the **heel** of the Saviour would be **scratched**, whereas the **head** of the Serpent would be **crushed**.

What is meant by the devil's "head"? Surely his most dread weapons - those things that comprise his chief power, and that spearhead his every attack: **sin, the law, death -**

<u>**Sin**</u>, Christ conquered by being made sin for us, that we might become the righteousness of God in him (2 Co 5:21).

<u>**The law**</u>, he conquered by fulfilling on our behalf its every demand, bearing the full weight of its fury upon his own body at Calvary, and so removing its penalty from us for ever (Ro 10:4; Ga 3:13).

<u>**Death**</u>, he conquered by righteously surrendering himself to it, and then shaking himself free from its awful enshrouding darkness, rising radiantly into God's light.

For three terrible days death held him a chained prisoner, but then, just as he had once loudly commanded the dead Lazarus to walk out of his tomb, so now again heaven rang with his shout, and the echo trembled in hell, as with a voice of thunder he cried, **"I LIVE!"** (Jn 11:25). Death shuddered. The bands began to break. Suddenly, resurrection and life broke through; Christ arose; the huge stone rumbled back - and gave Satan such a crack on the head as to leave him a dying cripple from that day to this!

Jesus has won!

And by his victory we too are made more than conquerors.

To those who believe in this Child of the woman comes the same promise our first parents received in the Garden. **God did not cast Adam and Eve away**; rather, he killed an animal and provided clothing for them. Likewise, the Father, through the death of his Son, has provided for us a glorious garment of righteousness.

God did not condemn that first couple - neither will he condemn you, if you cling to Christ.

God bruised Satan - thus creating a legal basis upon which he can ensure your conquest of every temptation, and restore to you all of the delights of Paradise.

God was with Christ in the darkness of Gethsemane and during the anguish of the cross - he will surely be with you in every time of trouble, in every long night.

God raised Christ in mighty power from the dead - so he is now able to lift you out of sickness and defeat, and to give you abundant life and perfect liberty.

The challenge is before us to believe this gospel fully, and to know that the Serpent's power is utterly broken - he bears a ghastly wound that is dragging him, sick and ruined, down to the pit. Let us no longer fear sin, or sickness, or death. See your enemy as God sees him, dejected and broken. Then, like the mighty war-horse when the trumpet of battle sounds, you too will laugh at fear, and your voice will eagerly shout, **"Ha! Ha!"** (Jb 39:22,25).

(II) WHY CHRIST CAME

There is an arresting sentence in the first letter of John -

> *"The reason the Son of God appeared was to destroy the works of the devil" (3:8)*

Language could not be plainer. We are here told exactly why Christ came. For this one powerful reason Christ was born: **to destroy the works of the devil.** Not for three reasons did Jesus come, nor even two. But for this one purpose he appeared among us: **to destroy the works of the devil!**

He came into this world to take up battle against the kingdom of darkness so that once and for all the question about whether iniquity or righteousness would prevail would be answered. He established the absolute supremacy of righteousness, and along with this opened up for fallen man a glorious new hope of freedom and happiness.

Now before examining just what Christ has achieved for us, it is necessary to understand what has **not** been achieved -

(A) SATAN IS NOT DESTROYED

Notice that Jesus appeared among us to destroy the **works** of the devil; but Satan **himself** will not be destroyed until the King returns in power and glory to establish his magnificent kingdom. Only then will the devil finally be caught and bound in the bottomless pit (Re 20:1-3). Until then, he remains free to roam the earth **"seeking someone to devour"** (1 Pe 5:8).

Therefore, whatever "destruction" Christ has wreaked upon the works of Satan falls short of actually purging those works from the face of the earth. That too will one day be fully done. But for the time being, the havoc wrought by Satan remains evident everywhere. In fact, scripture indicates, not only that evil will continue among men, but that it will reach a peak of frenzied virulence just prior to Christ's return -

> *"Woe to you, O earth and sea, for the devil has come down to you in great wrath, because he knows that his time is short!" (Re 12:12).*

In what sense, then, have the works of the devil been "destroyed"? Simply this: Christ has achieved for all who accept his great salvation a marvellous release from Satan's strength and authority. Thus we declare that in Christ we are -

(B) LOOSED FROM ALL BONDAGE

Those who have put their faith in Christ, who acknowledge him as their Lord and Saviour, can claim deliverance from, and victory over, every work of Satan in their lives. They can shake themselves free from every imprisoning bond. The key has been turned in the lock, the knots have been loosened, the links have been weakened.

The Greek word translated "destroy" (**luo**, from which our word "loose" is derived) means "to loose the grip of something," or "to render something not binding" - as ropes might be loosened, so that a prisoner can easily cast them aside; or as a father might loosen the bolts and nuts of a toy construction set, so that his small son can readily dismantle the model.

It is not so much that we ourselves are loosed from the works of Satan; rather, the thing that gave them strength has been removed, so that we may throw them off, as a child might break out of a paper bag.

But many Christians are like a circus elephant tethered by a light rope to a fragile peg. The great beast could easily snap its bond and walk away. But it once used to be tethered by a heavy chain fixed into a solid post. From that chain it could not escape. Now it has become so accustomed to being bound, or is so persuaded of the strength of its bond, it believes itself unable to break away. So it does not even try. Yet one tug would set it free!

In the same way, the people of God are held by wisps of straw, believing them to be invincible fetters.

Yet the scriptures are continually challenging us to step out of our prisons, just as the angel bade Peter to accept that his manacles were unlocked and to follow him to freedom through the open iron doors (Ac 12:6-11).

(C) LOOSED FROM WHAT?

At this point, people face the problem of determining what particular "works" may be attributed to Satan. How can we know what stems from God and what arises from our foe? The answer is easily found! If Christ came to destroy the works of the devil, then, to see clearly what is good and what is evil, we need only to examine the ministry of Jesus. Watching him in action, we soon learn what he established and what he overthrew!

What did Christ oppose? What did he always seek to destroy?

Using that as our criterion, we discover four battle fronts that comprise our enemy's main attack. The next chapter will expose those areas of satanic strategy, and show the glorious victory God has given us in Christ.

CHAPTER TWO:

SAVED TO THE UTTERMOST!

Before an enemy can be overcome he must be identified. The more you can learn about his weapons, his strategy, his location, and so on, the more likely your victory will be. The same rule applies to our conflict with the kingdom of darkness. Thus the previous chapter ended with the idea that we can recognise the works of Satan by looking at the things Christ opposed during his mission on earth. When that is done, we discover four battle fronts in our warfare with the devil -

(I) KNOW YOUR ENEMY

Whenever the powers of darkness wage war upon the saints, they do so by attacking them in one of these four ways -

(A) MORALLY - BY ENTICEMENT TO EVIL.

Despite the pervading optimism of the early part of this 20th century, modern man is being compelled bitterly to accept the dictum that sin is not simply a product of heredity, nor of faulty environment. We are not just the hapless victims of a bad confluence of genes, nor of an unsavoury upbringing. No one is fated to sin more than another. You are not destined to do wrong.

Sin is neither a genetic nor a social problem. It is a spiritual disease.

Men and women are at the same time responsible and not responsible for their sin. Insofar as we have all been born with a degree of spiritual corruption, the atonement of Christ covers our guilt. God does not condemn us for a sinful state for which we have no personal responsibility. But insofar as we have all, despite the most urgent protests of conscience, deliberately sinned over and over again, our guilt is scarlet. No remedy is left for us, except to flee to Calvary for protection and cleansing.

Christ was stringently opposed to sin. He had great love for people, but great hatred for their sin. At no time did he excuse sin as something they could neither help nor avoid. He demanded the highest level of purity and integrity:

> *"You must be perfect, as your heavenly Father is perfect!" (Mt 5:48).*

Sin, declared Christ, was a product of Satan's work (Jn 8:44), and it was his avowed aim to put away sin by the sacrifice of himself (He 9:26). He overcame and demolished sin, by submitting himself to it; then, through his resurrection he proved it had no power over him.

> *"For our sake, God made him to be sin who knew no sin, so that in him we might become the righteousness of God" (2 Co 5:21).*

Sin is transgression of the law of God. It is **everything** that makes you less than the best you can be. It is **anything** that brings you short of the glory of God. But whatever your guilt, by the giving of his life, the Saviour has gained your complete pardon.

But now he also offers you dynamic power to put sin to rout in your life (Ro 6:11-14). It is mockery to seek his pardon, while refusing to accept his power. You cannot truly gain **forgiveness** of sin unless you hunger equally for **freedom** from it. That is why Paul urges: "For freedom Christ has set you free; stand fast, therefore, and do not submit again to the yoke of bondage" (Ga 5:1).

(B) PHYSICALLY - BY INFLICTION OF DISEASE

Christ fiercely opposed sickness. Not once did he suggest that disease was the will of God. Wherever he went, usually the first thing he did was to heal the sick and cast out devils. Always he set himself to loose people from their infirmities; he yearned to set them free from their afflictions. He said that he had come to bring them a more abundant life. Only the devil, declared Jesus, came to hurt and kill.

So, by fighting sickness, Christ showed that in his opinion it came from the pit. It was one of the things he had come to destroy. When he met people who were crippled and diseased, Jesus said that Satan had bound them and they ought to be released (Lu 13:16). He came to heal those whom Satan had afflicted -

> *"God anointed Jesus of Nazareth with the Holy Spirit and with power, and he went about doing good and healing all who were oppressed by the devil"* (Ac 10:38).

Now it cannot be denied that Christ is still anointed by the Holy Spirit. Nor can it be denied that the one great aim of the Saviour is still to do good to men and women. Nor can it be denied that in Bible days this "doing good by the power of the Holy Spirit," and this "healing all who were oppressed by the devil," meant **healing all who were gripped by disease**. How then can it be denied that this same Christ, having the same anointing, and the same desire to do good, must be just as willing to heal the sick now as he was then? Christ is surely **against** your sickness; only the devil is **for** it!

Refuse then to capitulate to disease. Fight it with every means at your disposal. Especially fight it with the weapons of faith, for **"all things are possible if you believe!"**

(C) SPIRITUALLY - BY INDUCEMENT TO RITUAL.

With scorn and anger Jesus fought against the empty religion of his day. How sternly he spurned those religious leaders who claimed to believe the scriptures yet arrogantly fought against the power of God (Lu 11:19-20; Mt 22:29). Because they placed their traditions and dogmas above the scriptures (Mk 7:6-7), Jesus, with biting sarcasm, rejected them from the kingdom of God. They brought no healing to the people themselves, yet hated him because he did. He spoke to their face, and told them they were of their father the devil (Jn 8:44; and cp. Mt 23:1-33). It is hard to escape the conclusion that the Lord would say similar things to some modern church leaders.

The mere form of godliness has little worth if it is not coupled with the immediate power and authority of God (2 Ti 3:5). It is hardly enough just to go to church, sing a few hymns, be in the choir, have your name on a church roll, or subscribe to some creed or tradition. Scripture demands that we grip **Christ himself.** Every **real** Christian possesses the inward life of God, not just the outward show of religion!

We cannot be content merely to remember what Christ did twenty centuries ago - we need to see him doing the same things in our time. Of what use is it to know what Jesus **was** unless we also know him as he **is**? (Except that by discovering what he **was** we certainly do discover what he **is** - for he is **"the same yesterday, today, and for ever"** - He 13:8). Having seen him in action in the pages of the Bible, our faith should be stirred to see him in action in just the same way in our own lives.

What Christ was against in his day, he is still against today. The works he fought in ancient Palestine were of the devil, and those same works are still of the devil today. In fighting those Satanic works, Jesus healed the people physically, morally, and spiritually. He is surely willing to do just as much today, for you.

(D) INTELLECTUALLY - BY SEDUCTION INTO ERROR.

Perhaps the enemy is unable to find a place from which to attack you **morally**, **physically**, or **spiritually**, but he still has one more weapon, an attack on your **mind**. He will try to persuade you to believe false doctrine, to embrace error.

That was the first weapon he employed in the Garden of Eden, when he enticed Eve to doubt the truth of what God had said to her (Ge 3:1).

Some of the strongest warnings Jesus issued were spoken against those who either taught or accepted false doctrine: Mt 5:19; 7:15; 15:1-3,8-9; Lu 11:37-52; etc.

Paul warned about the severe judgment that would fall upon any person who erected a superstructure of false teaching upon the pure foundation of the gospel (1 Co 3:1-15; see also Cl 2:6-8; 2 Ti 2:15; 3:14; 4:1-4; Tit 2:1).

Each Christian has a solemn duty before the Lord to **"prove all (doctrines) and to hold fast only to that which is good"** (1 Th 5:21). This duty cannot be devolved onto any other person. It is your own responsibility to ensure you are hearing and receiving the truth of God. But in that task you have a sure ally in Christ, who is himself the Truth, and who gives to those who trust him the teaching Spirit. Hence John says -

> *"I write this to you about those who would deceive you; but the anointing which you received from him abides in you, and you have no need that any one should teach you; as his anointing teaches you about everything, and is true, and is no lie, just as it has taught you, abide in him" (1 Jn 2:27).*

In union with Christ, being filled with the Holy Spirit, immersing our minds and spirits in scripture, we are able to hold to the truth **"as it is in Jesus"** (Ep 4:21).

(E) OTHER WORKS OF SATAN

Scripture speaks of many other things Christ fought against, works of Satan he came to destroy. He always strove against the paralysing power of **fear**; he set himself to overthrow **death**; he warred against **doubt** and **unbelief**; he opposed **poverty** and **despair**.

By fighting against such things Jesus showed plainly what are the works of Satan and what are the works of God. He showed that God wants to pardon your sins and to heal your diseases; God wants to fill your life with joy and peace; God wants you to prosper and to be in good health; God wants to satisfy your deepest desires; God wants to deliver you from the grave and give you everlasting life.

For all of this Christ came. For all of this he now lives, ever making intercession for the saints, so that he might for all time utterly save those who draw near to God through him (He 7:25). The Greek word used in that verse is **panteles**. The clause in which it occurs could be translated in any of the following three ways -

(1) A Complete Salvation

"He is able to save to completion"

One of the fears people have is that life will pass them by, and leave them unfulfilled, their task incomplete, their potential unrealised. Undoubtedly that **is** the sad fate of millions who do go down to the grave disappointed and frustrated.

But that should never be the condition of a Christian. Christ is able to bring us to the full accomplishment of all God has planned for us in time and in eternity.

How can we who are led by the Holy Spirit, to whom the Spirit bears witness that we are the children of God, who cry **"Abba! Father!"** ever fall back into fear and slavery? (Ro 8:14-16).

How can we, being guided daily by the Lord himself, who is **"at work in us both to will and to do his good pleasure"** (Ph 2:13), ever feel that life is futile and empty?

To live with Christ is to live with a sense of destiny and of eternal purpose. It is to live with certainty that both in this life and in the coming kingdom, the God we love and serve is able, through the completed work of Christ, to bring each one of his servants to completeness. Indeed, in an imputed sense, this is already true of us: **"you have come to completeness of life in Christ"** (Cl 2:10); it but awaits the working of faith to make this fullness increasingly real in daily experience.

(2) An Eternal Salvation

"He is able to save for ever"

Do you remember the nursery rhyme?

> Pussy-cat, Pussy-cat, where have you been?
> I've been to London to visit the Queen.
> Pussy-cat, Pussy-cat, what did you there?
> I frightened a little mouse under her chair!

Now there was an animal that allowed itself to be distracted by a trifle. In the presence of royalty, he saw only a mouse. He missed the main event. He was diverted by a side show!

People are like that - so engrossed with the trivialities of time they miss the glories of eternity.

Jesus spoke often about the endless ages that lie ahead. He warned people not to become so busy with earth that they forget heaven. On the contrary, one of the marks of a true Christian is an eye for the coming kingdom of God. Peter says that we who truly believe cannot help but look continually for the new heaven and the new earth to come, in which only righteousness can dwell (2 Pe 3:13). Paul talks about the crown that belongs exclusively to all who love the day of Christ's appearing (1 Ti 4:8).

Whoever believes in Christ can never again imagine that the things of time are more real than the things of eternity. We live with a vision of the unseen, for we know that the visible things are transient, but the things that are unseen are eternal (2 Co 4:18).

(3) An Unchanging Salvation

"For all time he is able to save"

Christ came to show us God as he is, was, and always will be. What he has done before he can do again. What he was willing to do for his servants of old, he is willing to do for his servants today. We can do as David did when he was troubled - when he felt for a time that God had forsaken him - we can remind ourselves of all

God has done for his children in the past, and so stir up faith to believe he will do the same today (Ps 22:4-5).

This is all summed up in one word: **"Christ is able to save"** (Greek, **sozo**), a word with a wide meaning. **"Sozo"** embraces well-being of body, mind, and spirit. It is full deliverance of the whole person. It includes everything Jesus did for people in Bible days. That is exactly what this unchanging salvation still promises to believers today.[2]

(II) THE TRIUMPH OF THE CROSS

When and how did Christ destroy the works of the devil, and so make available to us this uttermost salvation? Paul gives an arresting answer -

> *"Christ disarmed the principalities and powers, and made a public example of them, triumphing over them in the cross"* (Cl 2:15)

The great battle between Christ and Satan took place at Calvary.

Righteousness and unrighteousness met there in open conflict.

Golgotha was the centre of that war between life and death.

There Satan (remembering the day, centuries before, when Christ had thrown him out of heaven) marshalled all his forces and thrust his full weaponry against the lonely Man on the cross. The powers of darkness fell upon the tortured Christ in a frenzy of hatred. The struggle was bitter and long. Two fierce cries reveal the desperate intensity of the conflict and the staggering burden Jesus was carrying: **"I thirst,"** and, **"My God, my God, why have you forsaken me?"**

But then came the triumphant shout of victory: **"IT IS FINISHED!"**

---

[2] You will find a more comprehensive discussion of the meaning of **sozo** in the VCC course, **Healing In The Whole Bible**.

Many years earlier the Lord had spoken through the prophet Isaiah and described this greatest battle of the ages. You can read about it in Isaiah 63:1-5. What enabled Christ to conquer? He cried: **"My fury, it upheld me!"** The fury of the Son of God! The fury of the Son of Man! The fury of God's Champion! With immense indignation he set himself against the ravaging forces of the devil and routed the dark armies.

Paul declared that the victory of Christ had three magnificent parts (Cl 2:15) -

(A) CHRIST DISARMED SATAN

In warfare the first spoils snatched from a defeated foe are his weapons and armaments. There are three powerful weapons Satan has used in his rampage against humanity. I described them earlier in this lesson. They are

- the thundering rod of the **law**
- the piercing dart of **sin**
- the cleaving sword of **death**

But the Saviour has now wrested those fearful weapons from the hands of the enemy. He nullified their power by breaking them across his own shoulders. The rod of the **law** vented its force against him on the cross and fell away exhausted. He allowed the dart of **sin** to pierce him deeply, but then he rose from the mire and crushed the power of evil. The sword of **death** struck him a seemingly mortal wound, but in three days he shook himself free from its grip, claimed the keys of death, and made the grave the gateway to heaven.

In the battles of ancient Rome the vanquished were stripped of their armour, their garments, their weapons; they were then chained together, and made to pass under a yoke to show their subjection and slavery. Even so has Christ disarmed our enemy and led captivity captive (Ep 4:8).

The word translated "disarmed" may also mean "to take away the enemy's treasure." Victors in a war impoverish and destroy the vanquished for two reasons: to prevent any retaliation by the enemy; and to increase their own wealth and prosperity.

So has Christ done for us. The Satanic kingdom is now broken and impoverished. The enemy staggers helpless like a ship at sea in a storm, its rigging shredded, its mast splintered (see Is 33:22-24). Christ and his kingdom are safe from any meaningful resumption of the war, and **"the treasures of darkness ... the hoards in secret places"** (Is 45:3) are now taken back to God.

The prophet saw well when he described his vision: **"prey and spoil in abundance will be divided"** - which means that the wealth the enemy gained in countless treacherous assaults now belongs to the servants of Christ. Even the "lame man" will have more than he can carry. No longer will the people say, **"I am sick;"** no longer will they fear the power of sin; for, because of the cross, **"they will be forgiven their iniquity"** (Is 33:23,24).

(B) CHRIST MADE A PUBLIC EXAMPLE OF SATAN

The highest honour a Roman general could receive was a decree from the Senate awarding him a "Triumph" in Rome itself. This was a special kind of victory procession. The victorious army paraded through the city, accompanied by a host of captives, the spoils of war, and great painted scenes of the battles it had won. A public holiday was declared, every house along the processional way was gaily decorated, and a million cheering people lined the streets for miles, applauding the mighty victors.

Here, for example, is the description given by Josephus of the "Triumph" of Vespasian and Titus, the two generals (father and son) who suppressed the Jewish rebellion and devastated Jerusalem in the war of AD 66/77[3] -

---

[3] This Roman victory was foretold by Jesus, 40 years earlier (Mt 24:1-2, 15-20; plus parallels in Mark and Luke).

"So (after the war) Titus took the journey he intended into Egypt ... (But) as for the leaders of the captives, Simon and John, with the other seven hundred men, whom he had selected out of the rest as being eminently tall and handsome of body, he gave order that they should be soon carried to Italy, for he had resolved to produce them in his triumph. So when he had had a prosperous voyage (he came finally to Rome) and the city behaved itself in his reception, for the people met him at a distance, as they had done in the case of his father (Vespasian).

"But what made the most splendid appearance in Titus' opinion was, when his father met him and received him; but still the multitude of the citizens conceived the greatest joy when they saw them together.... (so the people) determined to have but one triumph, that should be common to both of them, on account of the glorious exploits they had performed, although the senate had decreed each of them a separate triumph by himself.

"So when notice had been given beforehand of the day appointed for this pompous solemnity to be made ... not one of the immense multitude was left in the city, but everybody went out so far as to gain only a station where they might stand, and left only such passage as was necessary for those that were to be seen to go along it.

" ... And as soon as ever it was day, Vespasian and Titus came out crowned with laurel, and clothed in those ancient purple habits which were proper to their family ... Whereupon the soldiery made an acclamation of joy to them immediately, and all gave them attestations of their valour ... (and) when they had put on their triumphal garments, and had offered sacrifices to the gods that were placed at the

gate, they sent the triumph forward, and marched through the theatres, that they might be more easily seen by the multitude.

"Now it is impossible to describe the multitude of the shows as they deserve, and the magnificence of them all ... (for they) demonstrated the vastness of the dominions of the Romans; for there was here to be seen a mighty quantity of silver, and gold, and ivory, contrived into all sorts of things, and did not appear as carried along in pompous show only, but, as a man may say, running along like a river.

"Some parts were composed of the rarest purple hangings ... There were also precious stones that were transparent, some set in crowns of gold, and some in other ouches, as the workmen pleased; and of these such a vast number brought, that we could not but thence learn how vainly we imagine any of them to be rarities ... The images of the gods were also carried, being as well wonderful for their largeness, as made very artificially[4], and with great skill of the workmen; nor were any of these images of any other than very costly materials; and many species of animals were brought, every one in their own natural ornaments.

"The men also who brought every one of these shows were great multitudes, and adorned with purple garments, all over interwoven with gold ... Besides these, one might see that even the great number of the captives was not unadorned, while the variety that was in their garments, and their fine

---

[4]   That is, with great **artistry**, the original meaning of the word.

texture, concealed from sight the deformity of their bodies⁵.

"But what afforded the greatest surprise of all, was the structure of the pageants that were borne along ... for many of them were so made, that they were on three or even four stories, one above another. The magnificence also of their structure afforded one both pleasure and surprise; for upon many of them were laid carpets of gold. There was also wrought gold and ivory fastened about them all; and many resemblances of the war, and variety of contrivances, affording a most lively portraiture of itself; for there was to be seen a happy country laid waste, and entire squadrons of enemies slain ... **(Josephus here gives a description of these battle tableaux)** *... Now the workmanship of these representations was so magnificent ...that it exhibited what had been done to such as did not see it as if they had been there really present. On the top of every one of these pageants was placed the commander of the city that was taken, and the manner wherein he was taken.*

"Moreover, there followed those pageants a great number of ships; and for the other spoils, they were carried in great plenty. But for those that were taken in the temple of Jerusalem, they made the greatest figure of them all; that is, the golden table, of the weight of many talents; the candlestick also, that was made of gold ... After these spoils passed by a great many men, carrying the images of Victory, whose structure was entirely either of ivory

---

5   I suppose Josephus is referring to the custom of parading prisoners naked through the streets.

or of gold. After which Vespasian marched in the first place, and Titus followed him ...

"Now the last part of this pompous show was at the temple of Jupiter Capitolinus, whither, when they were come, they stood still; for it was the Roman's ancient custom to stay till somebody brought the news that the general of the enemy was slain. This general was Simon, the son of Gioras, who had then been led in this triumph among the captives; a rope had also been put upon his head, and he had been drawn into the proper place in the forum, and had withal been tormented by those that drew him along ... Accordingly, when it was related that there was an end to him, and all the people had set up a shout for joy, they then began to offer those sacrifices which they had consecrated ...

"And as for some of the spectators, the emperors entertained them at their own feast; and for all the rest there were noble preparations made for their feasting at home; for this was a festival day to the city of Rome, as celebrated for the victory obtained by their army over their enemies, for the end that was now put to their civil miseries, and for the commencement of their hopes of future prosperity and happiness."

In imagination, you should try to transfer that scene to the spiritual realm. Instead of Roman generals, visualise the triumphant Christ. In place of the pitiful Jewish captives and the tortured Simon, see the hosts of hell and Satan himself. And who but you can be numbered amongst those who receive the glad invitation to share in the spoils of victory?

Nor is this merely a picture of what will certainly happen when Christ returns and establishes his everlasting kingdom. No! It has

already happened! When Paul wrote **"Christ made a <u>public example</u> of the powers of darkness,"** he had in mind this very idea of a Roman "Triumph,[6]" and he declared that this procession had already been enacted at Calvary. There Christ made an open show of Satan. There he made a spectacle of the hosts of evil. There he held a cosmic "Triumph," witnessed by the assembled armies of heaven.

When Christ came down from the cross the world saw a dead, broken body; but heaven saw the Lord of glory - triumphant, immeasurably victorious, dragging the enemy host captive. When Christ proved invincible against Satan's power of death, by laying down his life only when the time had come (for his life could not be taken from him), every denizen of the kingdom of darkness knew that all hope of victory had gone. At that moment the captors became captives, and tyranny was ended!

(C) CHRIST TRIUMPHED OVER SATAN

If Christ so conquered at Calvary it was not for his own benefit but for ours. There was no need for Jesus to prove that **he** was Master over the devil. That had been proven ages before when, with a mighty arm, he had cast all of the fallen angels out of heaven and banished them from the glory of God.

The triumph Christ accomplished on the cross was a surrogate victory. Scripture challenges us to identify ourselves with the crucified One, by faith, so that all of the victory he gained may become ours. We are meant to join hands with Christ, and, marching on with him, to feel by faith the pull of the defeated armies as we drag them, beaten and broken, behind us!

---

6   The Greek word translated "example" is *deigmatizo* = "to make a public exhibition." Kittel says of its use in Cl 2:15, that it probably describes "the public display of the vanquished forces (of evil) before the cosmos, possibly in a triumphal procession." Lightfoot says the word means "displayed - as a victor displays his captives or trophies in a triumphal procession."

For us who believe, Satan is spoiled, Satan is shamed. His strength has been drained from him. He may tempt, but he can no longer compel you to obey his temptation. He may threaten, but he cannot destroy anyone who stands firm in Christ. The lion may roar, but his teeth are drawn; he can no longer devour. The serpent may hiss, but his poison has been nullified at Calvary. The dragon may belch smoke, but his fire has been quenched; he cannot sear anyone who clings to the cross.

(III) THE DEATH OF CHRIST

It is evident that the death of Christ is at the centre of Christian doctrine (Jn 12:27; 1 Co 1:18;2:2; etc.) Without the cross there can be no redemption for fallen humanity. There is no salvation without a crucified redeemer.

However, that view is not accepted by all who reckon themselves Christians. For example, in his book **"Honest to God,"** John Robinson wrote -

> *"The doctrine of the Atonement is not - as in the supranaturalist way of thinking - a highly mythological, and often rather dubious transaction between two parties, 'God' on the one hand and 'man' on the other, who have to be brought together, and which goes to explain, in Anselm's words, 'why God became man.' Much indeed of this mythological drama - such as the ransom paid to the Devil, or the notion that the Father punishes the Son in our place - is in any case a perversion of what the New Testament says. But, even when it is Christian in content, the whole schema of a Supernatural Being coming down from heaven to 'save' mankind from sin, in the way that a man might put his finger into a glass of water to rescue a struggling insect, is frankly incredible to man 'come of age,' who no*

> *longer believes in such a 'deus ex machina[7].' Yet church people continue to explain the Atonement in some such terms as this, picturing the interplay of two personified parties:*
>
> *'The relationship between God and man has been broken by original sin. Man could not pull himself up by his own shoe-strings, and thus the only hope of restoration was from God's side. Yet it was from our side that things had to be put right. It appeared hopeless. But God found an answer. For in Christ he himself became man, and as man reconciled us to himself.'"* [8]

Plainly, the bishop does not like that construction of NT teaching on the work of Christ. He is not impressed by its "supernatural" content. He reckons it does not represent NT teaching. Then he rather spoils his argument by descending to caricature, saying that atonement theory is like a man pulling an insect out of water. Then he partly rescues himself by showing that he does know what the "supranaturalists" teach - not that a man rescues the insect, but that the man becomes an insect (that is, God became man) to save the drowning creature. Then the bishop routs himself again by showing all too clearly that he will have nothing to do with any such proposition. But that is tantamount to saying he will have nothing to do with the New Testament; for, despite his disclaimer, it can scarcely be denied that the NT most certainly does present a

---

[7] Literally, "a god from a machine." The expression was used in old theatre to describe an intervention by God in a play, achieved by mechanical means. The phrase is now used to describe any "person, god, or event that comes just in time to solve a difficulty in a story, play, etc., especially when the coming is contrived or artificial" (World Book Dictionary). In theology it is used to describe a superficial view of Divine intervention in human affairs

[8] SCM Press Ltd. London, 1964; pg. 77,78.

theory of atonement based on the life, death, and resurrection of Immanuel, God with us!

Thus Leon Morris has written -

> *That the cross is of central importance to Christianity is clear even in the language we use. '**Crucial**' derives from a Latin word meaning 'pertaining to a cross,' and '**crux**' is simply Latin for '**cross**.' Whenever we say, 'The crux of the matter is this,' or, 'This is the crucial point,' we are saying, 'Just as the cross is central to Christianity, so is this point central to my argument.'*
>
> *" ... the theological centrality of the cross is seen in the structure of the Gospels, which have well been described as 'Passion narratives with extended introductions.' In each one the death and resurrection of Jesus take up a disproportionate amount of space. Everything is arranged to lead up to the climax of the cross. And Paul can sum up the Christian message in the words, 'We preach Christ crucified^9.' "*

A mass of evidence to confirm the centrality of the cross has already been given in other places in the Vision College curriculum, but at this point notice again the following -

(1) The death of Christ is of pre-eminent importance (Ga 6:14).

(2) Jesus willingly embraced the cross on which he would die (Mt 26:54).

(3) We too are called to identify ourselves willingly with Christ in his death and to undergo a spiritual crucifixion (Mt 16:24 ff; Ro 6:1 ff).

---

9   From an article in **Christianity Today**, April 17, 1987, pg. 23.

(4) Christ's death is called a ransom (1 Ti 2:6); an expiation (Ro 3:24-25); a sacrifice (He 7:27); an act of righteousness (Ro 5:18); an act of "divine magnetism" (Jn 12:32); a stumbling block (1 Co 1:23); folly (1 Co 1:23); the power and wisdom of God (1 Co 1:24)[10].

Think about each of the above descriptions of the death of Christ. What is the significance of each? Can you add to the list?

I allow that the life of Christ, the example he set for us, has a vital place in the gospel message, and that a significant part of our salvation depends upon allowing Christ to become incarnate in us day by day[11]. But I cannot evade the NT demand for me to begin at the cross; for it is there, and there alone that sin can be forgiven and new life discovered. With Paul, I delight to say:

> *"Far be it from me to glory except in the cross of our Lord Jesus Christ, by which the world has been crucified to me, and I to the world" (Ga 6:14).*

---

[10] The above list was compiled by Barry Chant, op. cit.
[11] See again the final lesson in the "Immanuel" series.

CHAPTER THREE:

THE POWER OF THE CROSS

There is power in the cross of Christ. The church is built around the cross. The cross is central to the Christian message. When preaching of the cross is removed from the church, Christianity becomes powerless, a collation of empty dogma, a hollow philosophy, unable to save people from their sins or to deliver them from their ills.

This theme is echoed right through the Bible, and indeed, throughout history. The tremendous changes wrought in human affairs, the mighty achievements of the gospel, all bear eloquent testimony to the power of the cross.

Men and women still fall at the foot of the cross and discover an instant miracle of pardon, peace, and joy. Still they throw their arms around the cross, and lo! their heavy burdens tumble away. Sick and broken people come to Golgotha's hill, look at the Christ who suffered there, and still find the priceless balm of God. Their diseases vanish like the morning mist. Out of the darkness and horror of Calvary, radiant light bursts like the morning glory!

What is the secret of the cross? What has given it such undiminished power over the centuries? What is it that enables men and women to find at Calvary the pardon, healing, and peace they can find nowhere else?

The answer can be expressed in one sentence: **the secret of Calvary's power is found in the sufferings of Calvary's Prince**. In the sufferings of the Son of God lies the heart of the full and great salvation God offers us in Christ. Every Easter should proclaim this message: Jesus suffered and died for our sins, and rose again from the dead, **so that we might be acquitted of all**

wrong-doing and set free to live abundantly under the blessing of God.

(I) THE SECRET OF CALVARY'S POWER

There remains mystery in the passion of Christ. No one has ever yet been able to fathom the infinite depths of Jesus' pain. He was indeed "the man of sorrows," and he stands unique in his sufferings. For this purpose he was born. For this purpose he lived. For this purpose he set his face steadfastly toward that ugly place just outside the walls of Jerusalem, known as "Skull Hill" (Golgotha).

The nearest we can ever come to an understanding of Christ's ordeal is to listen to the cries he made from the cross, while he was pouring his soul into death for us. Those expressions of anguish provide the only insight Jesus has given us into how he experienced death. Two cries in particular stand out. Both are stark and dreadful. Both show the awful depths of sin, and the glorious heights of salvation. They show us why at the cross we can find healing and forgiveness, and abundant supply of our every need. Those two cries are: **"I thirst!"** and, **"My God, my God, why have you forsaken me?"**

Mention of these cries was made in the previous chapter, but now the time has come to penetrate them more deeply. As I write, as you read, this prayer should whisper through every line -

> Oh, make me understand it,
>
> Help me to take it in,
>
> What it meant to thee,
>
> The Holy One,
>
> To bear away my sin.
>
>   - Katherine Kelly

(A) HE CRIED: "I THIRST!"

Incredibly, during that long night and violent day, this cry was the only indication Jesus gave of physical pain. For that very reason it shows how terrible was his pain at that moment.

Look back at the hours that went before. He had been deprived of sleep and nourishment; during a mocking trial, that was illegal in almost every part, he had suffered relentless questioning by the high priests; he had been buffeted by the soldiers, and flogged with the lacerating Roman lash (**"the shadow of death,"** the Romans called it, so brutal were the injuries it inflicted); the crown of thorns had been pressed into his head; punches and insults from the ranting crowds had assaulted him along the terrible road to **The Skull**; he even had to endure the rejection and curses of his dearest friends, who had denied him with oaths.

All of that he suffered without a murmur. But now, the bodily torture of the cross, and all that had gone before, wrung from his lips those two anguished words, "I thirst!" This was no ordinary thirst, such as that produced by a game in the hot sun. There is something dreadful in this sudden hoarse cry. It is as though every parameter of pain had suddenly shrunk down upon that one forsaken man.

His pain was physical; but even more, it was spiritual -

(1) Physical Pain

According to my wife's medical dictionary there are six varieties of wound: an **abrased** wound, where the skin is scraped off, such as by stumbling, or by carrying a rough object, or by a glancing blow; a **contused** wound, caused by a heavy blow; an **incised** wound, produced by a knife, spear, or other sharp instrument; a **lacerated** wound, where the flesh is torn open, leaving jagged edges; a **penetrating** wound, where the flesh is pierced right through; and a **punctured** wound, made by a pointed or spiked instrument.

The gospels and the prophets show that Jesus suffered all of those injuries. His enemies fell upon him in hate-filled savagery, and so mutilated him that

> *"his appearance was marred until he lost human semblance" (Is 52:14).*

Truly, he was

> *"wounded for our transgressions, and bruised for our iniquities."*

But that draws us on to contemplate the most awful part of his suffering -

(2) Spiritual Pain

While the cry "I thirst!" may be seen as the culmination of the outward violence he had suffered, it also marked a new depth in inner grief - far beyond anything Jesus had ever before experienced. It was a dreadful thirst for lost righteourness. It was the bruising, crushing weight of the sin of humanity descending upon him, along with the fevers of every sickness of every generation, and the sorrows of the whole human race.

That is what the Bible means when it says,

> *"For our sake God made him to be sin who knew no sin, so that in him we might become the righteousness of God" (2 Co 5:21).*

He who was the Son of God, equal with God, and the glory of all the heavens, stripped himself of his beauty and of his transcendent majesty, took upon himself human flesh, then humbled himself yet further to embrace the cross and the black squalor of human corruption. His purpose? To carry away from you and me the burdens that had all our lives held us in bands of sorrow.

What it meant to him, the indescribably holy, to enmesh himself with all that is unspeakable unholy, no language could ever tell. He experienced the rape of every pure virgin, the brutal slaughter of every innocent victim, the fierce pain of every ravaged body, the bitter poison of every guilt-wracked soul, the despairing sob of every bereaved heart - all of those things, and more; a blackness of sin past all measure, spanning all time and the whole vast universe, heaven, earth, and hell - all came to a focus in the dying, thirst-tormented Christ.

That is what the Bible means when it says,

> *"Surely he has borne our sicknesses and carried away our pains;"*

and again,

> *"Upon him was the chastisement that made us whole, and with his stripes we are healed;"*

and again,

> *"It was the will of the Lord to bruise him; he has made him sick ... for the Lord has laid on him the iniquity of us all" (Is 53:4-6,10).*

That is what the Bible means when it says,

> *"You know the grace of our Lord Jesus Christ, that though he was rich, yet for your sake he became poor, so that by his poverty you might become rich (2 Co 8:9).*

If you cannot measure the limits of the poverty Christ accepted at Calvary, a poverty marked by those bleak words of awful deprivation, "I thirst!" neither can you measure the limits of the pardon, healing, provision, and riches of grace the Father now wants to heap upon your life. His poverty has become the source of our wealth!

Finally, notice that John, who is the only evangelist who records that particular cry of Jesus (19:28), is also the only evangelist who records these other sayings of Christ:

> *"Whoever drinks of the water that I shall give him will never thirst; the water that I shall give him will*

> *become in him a spring of water welling up to eternal life ... He who believes in me, as the scripture has said, 'Out of his heart shall flow rivers of living water' " (4:14; 7:38).*

(B) HE CRIED: "MY GOD, MY GOD, WHY HAVE YOU FORSAKEN ME?"

Surely that is the most dreadful saying in the whole Bible. It shows that the Father had abandoned his only Son, had delivered him into the hands of his enemies, and had withdrawn heaven's support from him. For love of this world, God deserted Christ in his moment of deepest need.

It seems incredible that the complaint, **"Why?"** - with its tones of doubt and anxiety - should ever be on the lips of Jesus. But it does show the impenetrable mystery of the cross, and that in his incarnate state not even Jesus was fully able to comprehend what was happening to him and around him.

This cry is found first in the psalms (22:1), and Jesus, of course, knew it was there, and knew that one day he would speak it in fulfilment of scripture. I wonder if it disturbed him to know he would be driven to question the Father's purpose? I wonder if he sensed a mystery of darkness here that could not be revealed?

Perhaps this was part of his agony in the garden, when sweat was wrung from his brow like great drops of blood?

All else the prophets had spoken he was willing to bear with joy. But he shrank from the dread blackness, the infinity of pain, that reached out from the stark word - **"forsaken"**.

Facing that awful unknown, he three times begged, **"If it is possible, let this cup be taken away from me!"** Yet the Father's will could not be changed, and he yielded to it. Even so, when the grim moment came, its bitterness was so piercing, his anguished **"Why?"** sounded across the darkened skies - not in a staged fulfilment of prophecy, but in passionate urgency, torn from a heart engulfed in horror.

What was this blackness that engulfed him, that turned even the daylight into darkness, so that against his own desire he was compelled to raise a desolate complaint against the Father's desertion? We may discern here two things -

(1) The Deep of Sin

The ultimate issue of sin is to be God-forsaken. That is hell. No man has ever been there before or since. No other human being has ever yet been completely forsaken by God. Despite human wickedness, the Father has never ceased from drawing near to mankind in patience and mercy.

But when Jesus was made into sin on the cross, the Father in holiness had no choice but to withdraw utterly from him (cp. Ha 1:13). Jesus became the first man in history to be totally deprived of God. Probably not even Satan has yet been so forsaken.

Perhaps eventually demons and men who make sin their ultimate choice will suffer that ultimate isolation; but that hour has not yet come. At this time Jesus alone knows what it means to be <u>forsaken</u>.

So, in his hour of greatest need, he lost sweet consciousness of the presence of God, and he was left to struggle alone against the venom of sin, and alone to wage war against the kingdom of darkness. Surely hell will triumph? How can he, so solitary, his life ebbing away on the cross, hope to prevail against the assembled forces of evil?

There is an oracle in Isaiah that describes the annihilation of Israel's enemies, and it tells how the Lord got victory to himself. The scene is not Calvary. But the principles of Divine action are unchanging. So we may rightly see in that more ancient conflict a picture of what took place, when Christ wrestled with Satan and sin, and overcame them at the cross. You may have read this passage as part of the previous chapter, but look at it again -

Who is this who comes from Edom,

From Bozrah, with his garments crimson-stained?

Who is this, clothed in glory,

Who marches forward in mighty strength?

"It is I, announcing that righteousness will triumph,

I, who am strong to save!"

Why are your garments red,

Like the clothing of those who tread the winepress?

"I have trodden the winepress alone,

No man from any nation was with me;

So I trod down the nations in my rage,

I trampled them in my fury;

Their life-blood spattered my garments,

And it stained all my clothing.

"I looked for a helper, but could not find one;

I was astonished that no one supported me;

So my own arm brought me victory,

And I was upheld by my own anger!" (63:1-6).

Notice the exultant, almost wild, cry: **"My own anger upheld me!"**

The anger of the Son of God! The fury of the Lord of Righteousness! The wrath of the Eternal King! Who could withstand it? That blazing indignation against Satan gave him limitless strength. That searing rage forged in him a towering majesty, which made him invincible against even death. His fury exploded. He tore away the bands of darkness. He drove back his enemies. He trod them down and down. He smashed their weapons. Sin was absorbed and then dissipated. Sickness was grappled and then overcome. Unrighteousness fled. Righteousness returned. The presence of his Father was restored to him, and he knew that he had won!

His enemies, who had pinned him to the gibbet, alone and forsaken by God, fled in terror.

> *"He disarmed the principalities and powers and made a public example of them, triumphing over them in the cross" (Cl 2:15).*

Now an open door has been made for you and me to enter into the presence of God with joy. In the words of Peter:

> *"He himself bore our sins in his body on the tree, that we might die to sin and live to righteousness. By his wounds you have been healed" (1 Pe. 2:24).*

(2) The Deep of Sorrow

All sorrow is cause by an awareness of want. The sorrow of poverty is the want of money; the sorrow of weakness is the want of strength. **The ultimate sorrow is want of God.** That sorrow has not yet been forced upon any human being except Christ. There have been dark clouds, but never a complete deprivation of God. When Jesus experienced this he suffered the most pitiful sorrow in the history of the world.

Jeremiah caught a pale reflection of this deepest of all griefs in his Lamentation for Jerusalem, the city God forsook, yet still not so as he forsook Christ:

> *"Is it nothing to you, all you who pass by? Look and see if there is any sorrow like my sorrow which was brought upon me, which the Lord inflicted on the day of his fierce anger" (La 1:12).*

Christ endured this separation from God so that we might happily draw near to God. He took the pangs of eternal death so that we might have the prospect of eternal life. For this reason he is able to say:

> *"Come to me, all you who labor and are heavy laden, and I will give you rest"* (Mt 11:28).

That brings us to a third cry Jesus made from the cross - that magnificent, ringing cry of victory: "IT IS FINISHED!"

Yes! the work of redemption **is** finished. To all who believe in Christ, forgiveness, salvation, eternal life, come as God's free gift, along with a promise of healing of every sickness, comfort in every sorrow, supply of every need, and the daily abundant blessing of our mighty Lord!

In the presence of such grace, we can surely do no other than Paul, and declare: **"I am determined to know nothing among you except Jesus Christ, and him crucified"** (1 Co 2:2). In fact, Paul would say that you don't know anything worth knowing unless you know Christ crucified. For him, the crucified Christ represented -

(II) THE PINNACLE OF KNOWLEDGE

In that passage we hear a man saying he will believe nothing except what is true in the light of the cross; he will make no decision without first embracing the cross; in the face of every event and every fact he is determined to hold fast to Christ and to him crucified; Calvary will be the sole criterion by which he interprets every situation, every happening, every idea, that comes his way; he is going to place the crucified Christ between himself and everything he sees; he will throw the shadow of the cross over everything he experiences in the world.

Let us see what happens when Paul's motto is applied to some typical life-situations –

(A) IN THE FACE OF SIN

I am determined to know nothing except Christ and him crucified

We must face two facts:

> - the fact of our guilt before God (for "we have all sinned and come short of the glory of God"); and
> - the fact of Calvary.

If I contemplate only the first fact I will fall down in despair, undone, without hope or help in this world or the next. But if I place the cross in the scene and view my guilt from the perspective of Calvary - in other words, if I determine to recognise my guilt only in association with the greater fact of Christ crucified - what a change takes place! How the prospect is altered!

Because of my knowledge of the cross, I can now say -

(1) My Past Sin Cannot Accuse Me

Although many people do not recognise what is happening, much of human life is a quest for righteousness. People sense they are "unclean" and they yearn to be "clean". All the achievements of art and ambition have in them a strong element of restoring, or enhancing, man's good opinion of himself. We surround ourselves with beauty, we clutch at power, we strive for success, and all the time fail to perceive that what our restless spirits are really craving is righteousness.

But even when I recognise that my deepest need is to be cleansed from the filth of the spirit (not the filth of the flesh), where shall I look for righteousness? In myself? Hardly, for the deeper I peer into my own soul, the blacker the night I discover there. Perhaps then I can catch righteousness from my neighbour? How foolish; for as bad as I know myself to be I am yet sure that my neighbour is worse! Besides, the scripture says,

> *"Truly no man can ransom his brother, or give to God the price of his life" (Ps 49:7).*

Where then shall I look? Scripture replies: not on earth at all, but in the heavenlies, where Christ is, seated at the right hand of God (Cl 3:1-4). By the blood of the cross Christ has purchased complete remission of my sin, and given me the right to stand in peace with God. But this remission and this right have both been deposited in the heavenlies, far beyond spoliation by either man or devil.

How **Satan** would like to get hold of this new life of mine - but he cannot touch it, for it is hid with Christ in God.

Then imagine what my neighbour might do to this deposit of righteousness, if he had access to it. What accusations he might bring! What demands he might make!

But worse still, imagine what **I** might do to that sacred deposit myself, if I could only get my hands on it. How quickly I would turn it into a righteousness built on works instead of gifted by grace. How soon I would turn away from God's sacrifice and begin to trust in sacrifices of my own. How readily I would twist and spoil God's precious gift, if only God would give me opportunity to do so! Fortunately, he won't. The only righteousness I shall ever have, the only righteousness I shall ever need, is hidden in the heavenlies, eternally secure, eternally adequate, accessible only to faith; which itself must rest only on the cross and the Christ who there fulfilled on my behalf all of the law's righteous demands!

So long as I refuse to drift away from Christ, the crucified one, I know that not one past sin of mine shall ever have strength to accuse me successfully.

(2) My Present Sin Cannot Avert Me

Knowing Christ, and him crucified, I vigorously refuse to be paralysed by any sin that may still be with me, for I am free to take hold of the power of the cross and to step into the liberty that belongs to the sons of God. When I show faith in the cross, God at once acts to deliver me. God cannot ignore the death of his own Son, neither can he ignore me when I show resolution in holding to the cross. Christ steps into the lists on my behalf, takes his place as my Champion, and wrests victory from the enemy in my name.

That allusion to the old "trial by combat" provides a good illustration of what God has done for us in Christ.

"Trial by Combat," as a legal means of settling disputes, and of discriminating between innocent and guilty, was introduced into England by William the Conqueror. It presumed that when an accused person fought against his accuser in a duel, God would intervene to give victory to the innocent party.

However, two groups of citizens were exempt from combat: women and priests. The law provided that if a woman or a priest were accused they could appoint a "champion" to fight on their behalf. To the champion fell the task of establishing his sponsor's innocence and of defeating their common enemy. If the champion won, not only was the enemy routed (and often killed), but the whole realm then affirmed the innocence of the person who had been accused, and everybody rejoiced in the champion's vindication of his sponsor[12].

In like manner, Christ our Champion took the field for us. He destroyed our enemy. He vindicated us. He broke the strength of the kingdom of darkness, and now the whole creation is obliged, as we stand beside Christ, to declare us righteous.

Thus the cross not only nullifies every accusation that could have been brought against us, it also becomes the means by which we press home the advantage Christ has given us over our enemy. Satan's power is shattered, and we may repossess all that he stole from us, including even what we surrendered to him by our own folly and disobedience.

(3) My Future Sin Cannot Alarm Me

Many Christians are bold when they think about their past, and confident about their security today, but rather abashed when they

---

[12] There is an excellent description of this in Sir Walter Scott's novel, Ivanhoe, in which the hero champions the Jewish maiden Rebecca. The story is thrillingly told.

think about the future. They are not sure they will be equal to the demands life may make on them. They are apprehensive about backsliding. They feel that in the end they may fail and thus lose the grace of God; that after all they may still perish in sin, cut off from God for ever.

Those who think thus are simply showing they do not yet truly know Christ, and him crucified; for if they did, such alarms would never enter their minds.

We who have truly fused ourselves to the cross of Christ can never doubt that the same God who brought Christ to victory over sin **by way of the cross** will do the same for us. Christ was **made** sin; yet by clinging to the cross, by refusing each incitement to escape it, he disintegrated every vestige of that sin and rose to heaven's zenith crowned with beauty and glory.

Let us likewise bind ourselves to the cross by faith, refusing to let go of it, no matter what else we may do or what else may happen to us. The cross will then just as irresistibly become our stairway to paradise.

Another way to look at it is to imagine a weaker law being over-ruled by a stronger - as, for instance, the laws of aerodynamics allow a heavier-than-air machine to defy the usually inescapable laws of gravity. So, the law of sin is indeed mighty, and it has held humanity in cruel bondage for many generations; **but the law of the cross is mightier**. Stand where the cross stands, and you will stand on ground so secure, no power on earth or in hell will ever be able to disturb your spiritual serenity.

(B) IN THE FACE OF SICKNESS

I am determined to know nothing except Christ and him crucified

No one can deny the terrible fact of sickness in our community. Despite the wonderful achievements of medical science we all still live under the shadow of disease and pain. Every home is touched by it, every family is hurt by it; it is one of the most salient features of human life. Now, if I know these things only without the cross,

I might well tremble. But if I resolve to face sickness only in the knowledge of the cross, two wonderful things happen:

the dread of sickness vanishes like a night fog before the rising sun. The Saviour crucified means sickness conquered. It was the Father's pleasure to make him sick (Is 53:10, **lit.**) so that I might be well. At the cross he carried away my diseases and bore in his own body all my afflictions. He became the surrogate Sufferer for all who believe.

if sickness does happen to seize me, I am determined (because of the cross) not to consider the symptoms, but firmly to claim the promise of God. I confess that full healing is already mine, even as I ask God to grant me recovery from my illness (Mk 11:24; He 11:1; 1 Jn 5:14-15). I do not deny that the sickness exists, nor do I indulge in wishful thinking; but I do hold against every disease the greater fact of the crucified Physician. I know that as I maintain this affirmation, God will act on my behalf to make me whole[13].

(C) IN THE FACE OF A SCEPTICAL WORLD

I am determined to know nothing except Christ and him crucified

The world is sceptical of the message of the cross: intellectuals scorn it; the sophisticated despise it; the proud hate it; the sensual fear it; the materialistic reject it. It is often a hard thing to stand for Calvary in a world that is so antagonistic to everything the cross represents.

In the face of this sceptical world the Christian must decide to know only Christ, and him crucified. For it is true:

> *"The preaching of the cross is foolishness to those who are perishing; but to us who are saved, it is the power of God" (1 Co 1:18-25).*

---

[13] You will find a full discussion of the concept of healing in the Atonement in the VCC lesson series, Healing In The Whole Bible.

There is an old story about a railway workshop fitter who had been an alcoholic but now had become a Christian. His mates were astonished at the change in him, especially when they saw him reading a Bible during his lunch hour. They demanded he show them the story about Jesus turning water into wine, and jeered, did he actually believe in such miracles? The Bible was still an unfamiliar book to him, but with inspired wit he rejoined: "I don't know whether or not Jesus turned water into wine; but I do know that in my house he is turning wine into furniture!"

Likewise, we may not be able to debate on equal terms with all of our critics, and they may think they have won the day against us. But we cannot forget the scripture:

> *"It is written, I will destroy the wisdom of the wise, and the cleverness of the clever I will thwart ... For the foolishness of God is wiser than men, and the weakness of God is stronger than men" (vs. 19,25).*

Let the world say what it will, we know that **"the gospel is the power of God for salvation to every one who has faith"** (vs. 16). We have felt that power. What else then can we do, except continue boasting in the cross?

(D) IN THE FACE OF A COLLAPSING WORLD

I am determined to know nothing except Christ and him crucified.

We live in a time of upheaval and change. Few societies have been required to face such far-reaching transformation, or to undergo such radical re-structuring. Everything is being called into question. And along with many of our traditions, social mores, and much of our culture, the gospel is being rejected as an anachronism, an outmoded relic of an antiquated order.

But standing among this social collapse, this cultural destruction, this ethical morass, I cling to the cross because it shows two immutable things -

<u>Firstly</u>: God has once before intervened in history, at the end of an age, and he has promised to do so again (He 9:26-28).

God's program is on time, and there is no other power able either to hasten it or to delay it. This is my Father's world. It belongs to neither man nor Satan. The Father was prepared to send his Son to die for this world 20 centuries ago, and he will not forsake it now. Christ fulfilled the promise of scripture in his first advent; I cannot doubt he will fulfil the promise of scripture in his second advent. He came. He will come again. With joy we look forward to that splendid hour.

<u>Secondly</u>: God is always able to fulfil his own will; it is impossible for the purpose of God to be thwarted.

So the worst wrath of men and devils was helpless to prevent the safe coming of Jesus into this world. He was at one time the most fragile of creatures, a new-born babe at his mother's breast, but also the mightiest of the mighty, invincible. **"They sought the young child's life"** - but they were unable to harm even one of his hairs.

Quietly, unobtrusively, the Spirit of God guided Joseph and Mary, protecting the Infant, keeping him inviolate from all the devices of hell. Nor could they hinder him when he set himself to go to Jerusalem and to perish on the cross. He fulfilled his every intention. He died when he said he would - they could not kill him sooner, nor even later. He rose from the dead on the third day, as he said he would. Calvary thus became the symbol, not of ignominious defeat, but of overwhelming victory. The cross tells me that God has been, is, and always will be, able to fulfil his own will.

(E) IN THE FACE OF DEATH

I am determined to know nothing except Christ and him crucified

Jesus died as no other man has ever died. The scripture says, **"He poured out his soul unto death"** (Is 53:12). Who can understand this manner of dying? It was a death too dreadful to measure. It wrung from his soul the tortured lament that has already arrested our attention: **"My God, my God, why have you forsaken me?"**

We remember again that Christ was the only son of Adam to have been so wholly forsaken by God. During that direful hour he was utterly destitute. Once again we hear him declaim, with garments red, the awful words: **"I have trodden the winepress alone!"**

Upon such an astonishing drama we can only gaze with wonder. As the apostle wrote: **"God spared not his own Son, but delivered him up for us all"** (Ro 8:32). God spared him nothing - nothing of galling shame, desperate thirst, wracking pain, bleak despair, indescribable aloneness, nor of the crushing weight of sin, the burning hurt of disease, the bleak horror of death. All of this and more was unleashed against Christ as he poured out his life on the cross.

We die only in the shallows. Christ descended into the **lowest hell** and encountered death in its most fearsome abyss. But suddenly - he conquered! He fought death in its vilest form and emerged the victor. Light broke into the darkness. He arose. He ascended into heaven, leading captivity captive!

I am a man, and I must die. But bdcause of the cross there is nothing left in death for me to fear. Though I die, I shall surely live again. Because I know, and am determined to know only, Christ and him crucified, death has lost all sting. The Saviour's words are magnificently, delightfully true:

> *"Because I live, you will live also!" (Jn 14:19).*

SECTION TWO

THE CROWN

CHAPTER FOUR:

ALIVE FROM THE DEAD!

"Because I live, you will live also!"

Those resounding words have been echoing from the gospel for nearly 20 centuries. You would think by now they would have banished for ever from human hearts the spectre of the grave. Yet that gloomy place still haunts those who know they are dying. And still the urgent questions come: "Is death a full-stop, or merely a parenthesis? If I die, will I really live again?"

There are some people who find, or pretend to find, joy in the thought that death is an absolute end -

> We thank with brief thanksgiving
>
> Whatever gods may be
>
> That no life lives forever;
>
> That dead men rise up never ....
>
> - Swinburne (1837-1909)

Others disagree, who lack any hope of a future beyond the grave, and find no joy in the prospect, but only doleful resignation -

> Ah, make the most of what we yet may spend,
>
> Before we too into the Dust descend;
>
> Dust into Dust, and under Dust, to lie,
>
> Sans Wine, sans Song, sans Singer,
>
> and - sans End!
>
> - Omar Khayyam (Tr. Edward Fitzgerald)

And a similar bleak pessimism lies in the words of the seventh century Hindu poet, Bhartrihari -

> Now for a little while a child, and now
>
> An amorous youth; then for a season turned
>
> Into the wealthy householder; then stripped
>
> Of all his riches, with decrepit limbs
>
> And wrinkled frame, man creeps toward the end
>
> Of life's erratic course; and, like an actor,
>
> Passes behind Death's curtain out of view.

Then there are those, like William Henley, the late 19th century poet and editor, who shake a fist at both life and death -

> Out of the night that covers me,
>
> Black as the Pit from pole to pole,
>
> I thank whatever gods may be
>
> For my unconquerable soul ....
>
> Beyond this place of wrath and tears
>
> Looms but the Horror of the shade,
>
> And yet the menace of the years
>
> Finds and shall find me unafraid.
>
> It matters not how strait the gate,
>
> How charged with punishments the scroll
>
> I am the master of my fate:
>
> I am the captain of my soul.

Despite the passion of **Invictus**, and Henley's defiance of circumstance and chance, grim irony troubles every line - in the gloom, clutching pessimism waits to seize its prey. Henley cannot escape referring to the looming **"horror of the shade"** - in his deepest soul he knows that the grave mocks every proud pretence; the cemetery belies man's boast that his destiny is in his own hand.

Perhaps the sorriest of all mortals are those who neither rejoice in death, nor are resigned to it, but live rather in terror of it, haunted by its shadow, fearing its onslaught, dreading its possible aftermath. Their state is especially pitiable, as Publilius Syrus a century before Christ expressed in one of his maxims: **"The fear of death is more to be dreaded than death itself."**

But neither joy, nor despair, nor defiance, nor fear, are a proper response to the death that confronts us all.

Christ came to show us that the true way to handle death is with **faith** - faith that death is neither a thing to be welcomed nor dreaded, but simply accepted as a stage in the soul's progress toward God. The Christian sees in death only a parenthesis, a transition between life and life, a door between time and eternity. The resurrection of Christ has given mankind startling proof of the temporary quality of death. So John Donne sang 350 years ago -

> Death, be not proud, though some have called thee
>
> Mighty and dreadful, for thou art not so;
>
> For those whom thou think'st thou dost overthrow,
>
> Die not, poor death, nor yet canst thou kill me!
>
> One short sleep past, we wake eternally,
>
> And Death shall be no more:
>
> Death, thou shalt die!

Thus also the great apostle exulted: "Death is swallowed up in victory. O death, where is thy victory? O death, where is thy sting?" (1 Co 15:54-55).

So then, the same Bible that records Christ's death, with equal certainty records his resurrection from death, for without the empty tomb the cross would have been a futile sacrifice. The empty tomb stands with the cross at the very centre of Christian faith - cp. 2 Ti 2:8; 1 Co 15:1.

Barry Chant offers the saying: "The cross was the world's answer to Christ's life; the empty tomb was God's answer to his death[14]!"

It is not my intention to discuss all aspects of the resurrection of Christ; other authors have done that better than I can.[15] The notes that follow will instead give you a general introduction to the subject, followed by a discussion of what the statement "Jesus is alive?" means to each Christian personally.

I. THE NATURE OF THE RESURRECTION

The finest discussion in scripture of the resurrection is found in Paul's first letter to the Corinthians (15:1 ff)[16], where the apostle claims that we have hope of personal bodily resurrection only because Jesus was raised from the dead "in the body." His resurrection is the prototype of ours: as "he was sown a physical body, but was raised a spiritual body" (vs 44), so will our resurrection be.

What is a "spiritual body"?

It is obviously different from a normal body, for it is not "flesh and blood" (vs 49-50). But Jesus did describe his resurrection body as "flesh and bones," and he did say that the person the disciples

---

[14] Op. cit. The material on the next few pages is broadly based on the same unpublished text (pg. 37-43).

[15] Especially recommended are: Who Moved the Stone? by Frank Morison; Faber & Faber Ltd. London. This book, first published in 1930, is a classic. It contains a detailed analysis of the events surrounding the resurrection, demonstrates the reliability of the gospel accounts, and concludes that all of the evidence points irresistibly toward the actual, literal, rising of Jesus from the dead. It is still in print. Also: I Believe in The Resurrection, by G. E. Ladd; Hodder & Stoughton, 1975. A readable apologetic for the resurrection of Jesus, written to answer the question, "Can 'modern man' actually believe that Jesus rose from the grave?"

[16] Parts of this passage are explained in the VCC series on The Return of Christ.

could see was indubitably "Jesus himself" (Lu 24:39)[17]. It remains uncertain just how literally those descriptions still apply to Jesus, or how literally they will apply to us. But a general principle is plainly enough established: in the resurrection, identity of person is fully retained, while the risen body becomes subject to quite different laws of existence (cp. Lu 24:31; Jn 20:26-29).

Nonetheless, this "spiritual body" that emerges from the grave is clearly a body, not a spirit. It is not the disembodied ghost of popular fiction. It is substantial. It has form and shape. It can be physically handled, although it obviously transcends normal physical restraints.

So we may conclude that the body Jesus possessed when he stepped out of the tomb on that first Easter morning was his original body, although, through the processes of the resurrection, it was now transformed into a spiritual body. This is further demonstrated by the linen bandages and turban that were undisturbed by the resurrection (Jn 20:6-9; Lu 24:12; notice also, that the risen Christ could disguise his identity, and appeared to be

---

[17] It is usually suggested that "blood" is omitted from the risen body, because the blood is the "life" of the body in its corruptible state, in which it cannot inherit the kingdom of God (Ge 9:4; 1 Co 15:50).

clothed in ordinary working garments, despite leaving his grave-clothes in the tomb; Lu 24:15-16; Jn 20:14-15)[18].

---

[18] Chrysostom (late 4th century), in a sermon on Jn 19:16-18 made curious use of the idea of Jesus rising naked from the dead - he denounced lavish funerals!

"But do thou, when thou hearest that thy Lord arose naked, cease from thy madness about funerals; for what is the meaning of that superfluous and unprofitable expense, which brings much loss to the mourners, and no gain to the departed, or (if we must say that it brings anything) rather harm? For the costliness of burial hath often caused the breaking open of tombs, and hath caused him to be cast out naked and unburied, who had been buried with much care. But alas for vainglory! How great the tyranny which it exhibits even in sorrow! How great the folly!

Many, that this may not happen, having cut in pieces those fine clothes, and filled them with many spices, so that they may be doubly useless to those who would insult the dead, then commit them to the earth. Are not these the acts of madmen, of men beside themselves - to make a show of their ambition, and then to destroy it?

" 'Yea,' saith someone, 'it is in order that they may lie safely with the dead that we use all these contrivances.' Well then, if the robbers do not get them, will not the moths get them, and the worms? Or if the moths and the worms get them not, will not time, and the moisture of putrefaction destroy them?

"But let us suppose that neither tomb-breakers, nor moths, nor worms, nor time, nor anything else, destroy what lies in the tomb, but that the body itself remains untouched until the Resurrection, and these things are preserved new and fresh and fine; what advantage is there from this to the departed, when the body is raised naked **(as Jesus was)**, while these remain here, and profit us nothing for those accounts that must be given?

" ... And this I say not as taking away the custom of burial (that be far from me), but as cutting short its extravagance and unseasonable vanity.

64

Further speculation on the nature of the resurrection, beyond what Paul suggests in his letter to the Corinthians, seems futile. We cannot know just how the resurrection of Jesus occurred; nor can we define with any precision what may be his present human form in heaven. But we **can** affirm that Jesus did rise bodily from the grave, in human form, and that this miracle was not wrought for his sake, but for **ours**. If the resurrection had been only a

---

" 'But,' saith someone, 'feeling and grief and sympathy for the departed persuade to this practice.' The practice doth not proceed from sympathy for the departed, but from vainglory. Since if thou desirest to sympathise with the dead, I will show thee another way of mourning, and will teach thee to put on him garments which shall rise again with him, and make him glorious. For these garments are not consumed by worms, nor wasted by time, nor stolen by tomb-breakers. Of what sort then are these? The clothing of alms- doing ... **(etc)** ... These (garments) make men distinguished, these make them glorious, these place them in safety; but those used now are only something for moths to consume, and a table for worms.

"And this I say, not forbidding to use funeral observance, but bidding you to do it with moderation, so as to cover the body, and not commit it naked to the earth. For if while living (Christ) biddeth us have no more than enough to cover us, much more when dead, since the dead body hath not so much need of garments as when it is living and breathing ...

" 'But the onlookers will laugh,' saith someone. Most certainly if there be any laughter, we need not care much for one so exceedingly foolish; but at present there are many who rather admire and accept our true wisdom. For these are not the things which deserve laughter, but those which we do at present, weeping, and wailing ... those things deserve ridicule and punishment.

"But to show true wisdom, both in these respects, and in the modesty of the attire used, prepares crowns and praises for us, and all will applaud us, and will admire the power of Christ, and will say, 'Amazing! How great is the power of the Crucified One! He hath persuaded those who are perishing and wasting, that death is not death; they therefore do not act as perishing men, but as men who send the dead before them to a distant and better dwelling-place. He hath persuaded them that this corruptible and earthy body shall put on a garment more glorious than silk or cloth of gold; therefore they are not very anxious about their burial, but deem a virtuous life to be an admirable winding-sheet!'

vindication of Jesus himself, it might well have been dispensed with - what need has he to be encumbered with a human form in heaven?

But it was much more than that.

If the work of Christ had been finalised on the cross, so that nothing remained for him to do except joyfully to resume his throne in heaven, knowing that his mission was perfectly accomplished, then a bodily resurrection would have been unnecessary. He could have left his body behind and simply returned to heaven **spiritually**. But scripture makes it plain that the work of redemption was not completed at the cross. The last part of it depended on Christ rising **bodily** from the tomb. If he had not been so raised, then our faith would be futile, and we would still be in our sins! (1 Co 15:17).

I will explain later the various ways in which Christ's resurrection is an integral part of our salvation. But for now let it be noted that this redemptive aspect of his resurrection places it into a unique category. No other person has ever risen from the dead as Jesus did. His resurrection was not merely the kind of **resuscitation** that others have experienced when they were raised from the dead by the power of God - for their resumption of life was only temporary. Like Lazarus, they lived only to die again. But this Man lives for ever! (He 7:24-25; 10:12-13). The resurrection of Jesus was an utterly new event, unparalleled in history, dynamic in its power, almost incredible in its consequences!

II. THE EVIDENCE FOR THE RESURRECTION

What evidence is there for the resurrection of Jesus of Nazareth? How can we be sure that he is the only one who ever succeeded in shaking off the bands of death?

That question is not really about whether or not Jesus actually did rise, but rather about the reliability of the witnesses who report his resurrection - that is, the apostles. Belief in the resurrection begins with the accuracy of the NT documents, especially the gospels. There are three responses people make to that claim -

1. Acceptance

Millions of Christians are persuaded that the NT is authentic and accurate, an inspired revelation from God. For them the NT speaks with divine authority; therefore, the witness the four gospels give that Jesus, after lying in the tomb for three days, rose from the dead, must be accepted as plain truth.

2. Rejection

There are probably millions of other people who reject the NT simply because it **does** tell the story of Jesus rising from the dead. For them it is axiomatic that no one can overcome death; hence, any witness who says that he saw a resurrected man must either be deceived, or a deceiver. Others deny that Jesus rose from the dead on the grounds that the story is a mythical accretion to the original gospel; in other words, they dispute the integrity of our present NT documents.

3. Neutrality

These people announce that they intend to maintain an attitude of neutrality. They will neither accept nor reject the gospel story until more proof can be presented. But at once they face a peculiar problem: there is no possibility (nor has there ever been) of **proving beyond all doubt** that Christ actually did rise from the dead! The "proofs" of his resurrection are "infallible" (Ac 1:3, KJV) only to those who are disposed to believe them. Not even in Bible days was it possible to "prove" to a secular mind that Christ had walked out of his own tomb, in the sense that you could "prove" that Caesar was still alive and ruling the Roman empire.

More than 500 people claimed to have seen the risen Christ (1 Co 15:3-8); but even today, if 1000 people said they had seen alive a man who was known to have been hanged and to have been definitely dead, they would not be believed - unless the former dead man remained continually visible and accessible to anybody who wanted proof that he really had shaken off death. But that is just what Jesus did **not** do.

His post-resurrection appearances were highly selective. He never intended to provide evidence of his resurrection that would be unassailable by even the most sceptical mind. He was concerned primarily to satisfy those who were being called by the Father to eternal life.

Does that mean there is **no** proof of the resurrection we can offer to a sincere inquirer? Of course not. There are some powerful historical evidences of Jesus' triumph over death: we have those more than 500 eye-witnesses, who certainly saw **something**; there is the witness of the church itself, whose very existence is all but inexplicable apart from the resurrection; and there is the testimony of millions today who claim that Christ is as real to them as if he were visibly standing beside them.

Those evidences, and others, are discussed in more detail below. But notice first -

(A). AN INVALID NEUTRALITY

1. Evidence Must Be Faced

Since there is at least **some** easily found historical and objective proof that Jesus did rise from the dead, a neutral attitude becomes essentially dishonest. The testimony must be reckoned with. It may be rejected, but it cannot just be ignored - for it is the only available testimony, and there never will be any more (until Jesus himself returns in glory).

So the person who claims to have a neutral attitude is in fact camouflaging an actual rejection of the evidence. He is saying that he refuses to listen to the only witnesses we have, or can have.

The fact is, no-one can **fully** validate historically, or objectively, either that Jesus **did** or did **not** rise from the dead. In the end, people accept or reject the resurrection for subjective reasons - that is, either because they are moved toward faith; or else because they decline to believe that a man **can** rise from the dead, no matter what evidence is produced.

The biblical attitude is simply this: **anyone whose heart is open to God will be given an overwhelming witness that Christ is alive.** To them the "proofs" will indeed be "infallible". With joy they believe, and in believing, personally discover the risen Christ. He shows himself alive to them. He makes his dwelling within them, lighting in them the glory of God[19].

2. An Ancient Objection

Nothing more than that a certain Galilean preacher had by some extraordinary power overcome death.

It could not show that this Jesus was the eternal Son of God; it could not show that his death and resurrection were part of a divine process of redemption for dying humanity; it could not show that this Man has power to give pardon and eternal life to all who trust in him; and so on.

All of those things would remain accessible to faith alone (just as they are now), to be believed or disbelieved according to the disposition of each person.

How can God "prove" to every person that the risen Christ is Saviour and Lord of all the earth, except by such a demonstration of awesome power that all personal volition would be removed from mankind? And then, how often would that demonstration have to be repeated? Each day? Each month? Each year? And how then would men and women be other than iron-bound slaves? What opportunity would anyone have to develop genuine loving faith, and deep intimate fellowship with the Father?

---

[19] On these matters, see again the fuller discussion in the VCC series on **The Authenticity & Authority of the Bible**, and **The Return of Christ.**

3. An Unfair Advantage?

It may be objected: "What about those to whom Jesus actually did show himself? Were they not given an unfair advantage? Was not <u>their</u> freedom of choice taken away?"

The answer is simple: human nature being what it is, as time went by the disciples' remembrance of what they had seen must have grown dim. And as persecution grew more fierce, and they were faced with the choice of denying Christ or perishing miserably, even **their** assurance that Christ had conquered death must have needed the bolstering only faith can give. Mere remembrance must have become increasingly inadequate.

After all, there had been only a few appearances of the risen Christ, to comparatively few people.

In the end, the faith of each of the early disciples in Jesus' resurrection had to be based on the same foundations as ours is: **(a)** the supportive testimony of the other eye-witnesses; **(b)** the predictions of the OT; **(c)** the promise of Jesus; and **(d)** the witness of the Holy Spirit, confirming personally within each believer, and by his works in the church, that Christ is indeed our living Saviour and Lord.

4. The Only Possible Way

When you think about these things, you realise that the gentle way in which God from the beginning has testified that Christ is alive is the only way he could have done so. For those who are willing to believe, the proof is adequate; for those who are unwilling to believe, no amount of proof, no display of Divine majesty, could turn their treason into trust. The Lord might cower them by force, but he could not convert them. They might become his captives, but they would never be his children. Jesus himself recognised this principle -

> *Judas (not the one known as Iscariot) asked Jesus: "Lord, tell us why you are revealing yourself to us, but hiding yourself from the world?" Jesus replied:*

> *"Everyone who loves me will believe the things I have said, and my Father will in turn love them, and we will come and dwell with them" (Jn 14:22-23).*

So then, since the Father's desire is to lead **"many sons to glory"** (He 2:10), he has chosen to follow for as long as he can the pathway of gentle persuasion. It is the same now as it was in the beginning: **"Whoever will, may come!"** (Re 22:17).

However, the above remarks are not intended to weaken the historical aspect of the resurrection. If Christ is **"here"** today, it is only because he was not **"there"** in the tomb on that first Easter Sunday (cp. Mt 28:6). The historical foundations of the resurrection cannot be denied without quickly destroying confidence in the promise:

> *"All power in heaven and on earth has been given to me ... and lo, I am with you always, even to the end of the world!"*

Jesus did not survive death in a merely spiritual sense (as any righteous person might do), he actually rose from the dead **physically**, in an utterly unique and marvellous display of strength, which has now become the guarantee that **all** the dead will likewise rise.

Let us then examine the evidence for this mighty event -

(B. THE PRE-RESURRECTION WITNESSES

1. General O.T. References

There are intimations of the resurrection of Jesus in the OT:

> *"Thou dost not give me up to Sheol, nor let thy holy one see the Pit" (Ps 16:10; cp. Ac 2:25-28; see also Ps 49:15).*

> *"Thou dost lay me in the dust of death ... Deliver my soul from the sword, my life from the power of the*

> *dog" (Ps 22:15,20; see also the whole psalm with its strong messianic content.)*
>
> *"I will divide him a portion with the great, and he shall divide the spoil with the strong, because he poured out his soul to death ... " (Is 53:10-12).*
>
> *"Jonah was in the belly of the fish three days and three nights ... " (Jo 1:17; 2:10; cp. Mt 12:40).*
>
> *"The stone which the builders rejected has become the capstone" (Ps 118:22-24; cp. Mt 21:42).*
>
> *"You are my son, today have I begotten you" (Ps 2:7; cp. Ac 13:33; He 1:5; 5:5).*

Upon such references as those Jesus built his own confidence that the grave could not hold him. He knew **"from the scriptures"** (1 Co 15:3-4) that he would be put to death, but would just as certainly rise again - see Mt 20:18-19; Mk 9:30-32; 10:33-34; Lu 9:22; 18:31-34; 24:7, and especially verse 46,

> *"He said to them,* Thus it is written, *that the Christ should suffer and on the third day rise from the dead."*

Other OT references that would have encouraged his faith in the resurrection may have been: Jb 14:12-15; 19:25-27; Ps 17:15; Is 25:8; 26:19; Da 12:2,3,13; Ho 13:14.

2. On The Third Day

Jesus' confidence that he would rise on the "third" day would have been built not only on the story of Jonah, but also on other **"third day"** references. These prophetic intimations often seem very tenuous to western minds. But numbers in the Bible frequently have much deeper significance than we are prone to see in them. Hence W. M. Smith, quoting Philip Schaff, writes,

" 'The biblical symbolism of numbers is worthy of more serious attention than it has received in English theology' ... **(then Smith**

continues) ... Possibly the most specific reference (which could be taken by Jesus as predicting his resurrection on the third day) ... was the confidence of the remnant of Israel, 'After two days he will revive us; on the third day he will raise us up, that we may live before him' (Ho 6:2) ... The very first occurrence of the word ('three') in the Bible - and generally first occurrences of basic words in the Bible have great meaning - is relevant to the subject, for it is on 'the third day' (Ge 1:9-13) that biological life first appeared".[20]

Smith finds other **"third day"** examples in: Joseph's prediction that Pharaoh's butler would be released from prison on the third day (Ge 40:12,13); the release of Joseph's brothers after three days (42:17, and notice the wording of vs 18); the plague of darkness endured for three days (Ex 10:22-23); punishment periods of three years (2 Sa 21:1; 1 Kg 17:1; 18:1); and the command not to keep the remains of animal sacrifice beyond three days (Le 7:17,18; 19:6-7).

In those places the number 3 is associated with punishment, the darkness of separation, and the salvation of a righteous remnant. Since Jesus was a Jew, reared in a Jewish environment, the significance of the number 3 would have been important to him, in such a way he had no doubt at all **"the scriptures"** taught that he would lie in the grave only three days (Jn 2:19,21; Mt 12:40; 16:21 and parallels; 17:23, with Mk 9:31; and Mt 20:19, and parallels; Lu 24:7).

The Jewish leaders were aware of the manner in which Jesus had applied the prophecies to himself, and of his own bold prediction, often repeated, that he would rise from the dead on the third day. So they took extraordinary precautions to guard against fraud (Mt 27:62-24). Instead of insisting that his body be thrown into

---

[20] Article, **The Third Day**, <u>Pictorial Encyclopedia of the Bible</u>, ed. M.C.Tenney, Zondervan Publishing House, Michigan; Vol. 5, pg. 700; 1975.

Hinnom[21] along with the other malefactors, they gave permission for him to be buried in Joseph's tomb (Mt 27:57-60). The fact that this was a newly dug tomb, hewn out of solid rock, and therefore free from ancient secret passages, may have encouraged the authorities to give this permission. But they made doubly sure by sealing a great stone across the face of the tomb, and then mounting a guard of soldiers. Thus they hoped to prevent his disciples from snatching away the body, and then pretending that Jesus had risen from the dead. Their precautions were in vain. By the third day the tomb was empty. Where was Jesus? The unanimous witness of the first Christians is that he was alive again. He had risen!

C. POST RESURRECTION WITNESSES

1. Paul

The writings of Paul present a very early witness of the resurrection. For example, Paul gives a list of resurrection appearances in 1 Co 15:3-8. This letter was written about 55 A.D., but the list of appearances had already been given to the Corinthians verbally some 5 years before (vs 1-3). Some of the information in this list Paul probably got (vs 3) when he visited Peter and James in Jerusalem, about A.D. 40 (e.g. the information about James, vs 7; see also Ga 1:18-19).

So this evidence dates from a time less than ten years after the resurrection happened. Moreover, Paul says that most of his witnesses were still living when he wrote his letter (vs 6). Scholars of all colours, from ardent fundamentalists to cool liberals, number the first letter to the Corinthians among the undisputed writings of Paul. So the testimony contained in this passage, authentic and ancient, is quite powerful.

---

[21] Hinnom was a continually burning rubbish dump, in a valley adjacent to Jerusalem. It was used also as a burial place for animals and criminals. It became a symbol of hell.

2. Mark

The apostle Mark is another early witness. His gospel almost certainly pre-dates those of Matthew and Luke. Mark probably gained his knowledge about the life of Christ from Peter, but he was apparently an eye-witness of Jesus' death and resurrection. Quite likely he was the **"young man"** who was in the Garden when Jesus was arrested (Mk 14:51-52), and who was also at the tomb on the resurrection morning (16:5)[22].

In any case, Mark is one of the earliest witnesses to the resurrection. His gospel was written some 30 years after the resurrection, but it was built on a strong oral tradition that had become entrenched among the churches many years earlier.

3. The 500 and others

Let us go back to Paul's list of witnesses, and look more carefully at each of them (1 Co 15:5-8).

Prior to his crucifixion Jesus told his disciples he would rise from the dead, and would show himself only to them. He also told them why this would be so -

> *"In just a little while I will be gone from the world ... (but) when I come back to life again, you will know that I am in my Father, and you in me, and I in you. The one who obeys me is the one who loves me ... and I will reveal myself to him.*
>
> *"(His disciples) said to him, 'Sir, why are you going to reveal yourself only to us disciples and not to the world at large?'*

---

[22] Other commentators prefer to identify the **"young man"** at the tomb as an angel (not Mark), in harmony with Mt 28:2-7. This also appears to be the opinion of the author of the apocryphal **Gospel of Peter** (c. 150 A.D.), who combines the accounts of Matthew and Mark: " ... they found the tomb opened ... and they saw there a certain young man sitting in the midst of the tomb, beautiful and clothed in a robe exceeding bright."

> *"Jesus replied, 'Because I will only reveal myself to those who love me and obey me. The Father will love them too, and we will come and live with them'* " *(Jn 14:19-23, Living Bible).*

Thus we are told why the risen Christ veiled himself from everyone except those who had been chosen to be his witnesses (see also Ac 10:40-41). Even so there were more than 500 of those people. Paul lists them as: **Cephas, The Twelve, more than 500 brethren, James, all the apostles, and Paul himself.** All of these found the evidence of the resurrection to be convincing. It may not have been "scientific" evidence (the kind demanded by sceptics); but, even supposing such evidence was possible for a **spiritual event** like the resurrection, God had no interest in providing it.

If the resurrection had been nothing more than the resuscitation of a corpse, then it would have been easy to prove it irrefutably to anyone with ordinary perceptions. But (as I began to suggest a few pages back) how could an event such as the resurrection, which was unique in character, which represented a wholly **new** mode of being, and which was essentially spiritual, be objectively proved to a sceptic without in the process destroying his volition?

Physical sense alone cannot discern the risen Christ. He must be spiritually perceived. He cannot be discovered by mere intellectual effort, but must be found by faith. Apart from compulsion, which God will not use, only those with the right kind of eyes can truly see Christ.

So the evidence of the resurrection was not intended to convince scientists, nor even historians, **but to provoke faith in those whom Christ had chosen to be his witnesses.** For them it was stunningly effective; so much so, that not even the most barbaric and unendurable tortures could persuade them to deny their allegiance to Christ.

Remember that the original disciples were all people who at first derided the very idea of Jesus rising from the dead. Nothing seemed to them more improbable - Mk 16:1-5,8,11-14; Lu 24:1-4,11,25,37-41; Jn 20:1-2,9,13-15,25; and cp. Ac 26:24[23]. But they were also Jesus' friends. They had known him in the flesh. No others were so well qualified to recognise that the **risen** Christ was indeed the **same** person as the one whom they had loved. No others would have been so suspicious of a possible impostor, nor could have so readily recognised a fraud.

But once their doubts had been removed they joyfully proclaimed that this risen Man was indeed Jesus. No change in identity had occurred. Their Lord himself had truly been restored to them, although his body had taken on a strange spiritual quality.

When that fact had been established among his friends there was no longer any necessity for Christ to appear in bodily form (the one exception was Paul, **"as to one untimely born"**). Jesus' post-resurrection appearances had achieved their purpose. The only thing remaining was for the witnesses to bear witness.

How they did that, and who those first witnesses were, is the theme of the next chapter.

---

[23] The OT predictions of Messiah's death and resurrection became clear to them only after the event.

CHAPTER FIVE:

WITNESSES OF THE RESURRECTION

> By thine Agony and bloody Sweat;
>
> By thy Cross and Passion;
>
> By thy precious death and Burial;
>
> By thy glorious Resurrection and Ascension;
>
> And by the coming of the Holy Ghost,
>
> Good Lord, deliver us!
>
> - from the Prayer Book of 1662

The ancient recital recognised that for us Christians there can be no deliverance apart from **"the glorious resurrection"** of Christ our Saviour. **"If Christ has not been raised from the dead,"** said Paul, **"then our preaching is worthless, and so is your faith. More than that, we become the most miserable of men!"** (see 1 Co 15:12-19).

But of course Paul had no doubt about the matter. He **knew** that Christ was alive from the dead. Why was he so confident? Because he was able to call upon a group of eye-witnesses whose testimony he was confident could be trusted ....

(I) THEY SAW HIM ALIVE!

Your previous lesson closed with a reference to the list Paul gives of those eye-witnesses in 1 Co 15:5-8; and the first of them is -

(1) Cephas

Cephas, of course, was Peter. The name means "a rock", and it was the personal name given to Peter by Jesus. Yet how sadly he failed to be that rock. When Jesus most needed the support of his friends, Peter denied his Lord with curses. But with infinite love Christ allowed Peter to be first among the apostles to confirm that he was risen from the dead (Jn 20:4-8. There is also another private appearance to Peter recorded in Lu 24:34, but no other details of this are given in the NT).

It is hard to see how anything other than undeniable proof that Christ really was alive again could have changed the timorous Peter into the rock-like Cephas. His transformation from cowardice to courage is astonishing. The disciples themselves boldly attributed this transformation to an indisputable fact: their Lord had conquered death (Ac 4:1-3,8-10).

(2) The Twelve

The appearance to the twelve is described in Jn 20:19-29. A notable aspect of this appearance is its link with the giving of the Holy Spirit (vs 22). This was a favourite theme of John. In several places he draws special attention to Jesus' promise that the Holy Spirit would be sent to the disciples after his resurrection - see 7:39; 14:16,18,19,26,28,29; 15:26; 16:7,16.

The day of Pentecost thus became for the disciples absolutely conclusive proof that they had not been deluded by spurious apparitions of the risen Christ. They had not been dreaming, nor hallucinating. They really had seen him. And now, in fulfilment of his own promise, the Holy Spirit was poured out upon them (Ac 1:4-5,8). Their pentecostal experience powerfully confirmed to them that Jesus had indeed been **"raised up by God"** and that he was now **"exalted at the right hand of God"** (Ac 2:32-33).

The same proof is offered to us today.

If anyone is disposed to doubt that Christ is alive, let him consider the multiplied millions of people who have themselves enjoyed a personal pentecost during this 20th century! Every person who is baptised in the Holy Spirit becomes a living demonstration that Christ is alive! Every time I hear myself, or others, speaking in tongues by the power of the Holy Spirit, I know that Christ is still seated at the Father's right hand, and that he is still **"pouring out this which I see and hear"** (Ac 2:33)!

Glossolalia is a resurrection anthem! It is a symphony of eternal life created by the Ever-living Christ!

(3) The 500 Brethren

There is no actual description of this appearance anywhere in the NT, although it is generally thought that it took place on a mountain in Galilee - see Mt 28:7,10; also 26:32; Mk 14:28; 16:7. At the time Paul wrote, most of those 500 witnesses were still alive, and some of them may well have been personally known to the Corinthians.

There are three ways of approaching this claim:

1. it could be argued that **"the 500 brethren"** were fictitious, invented either by Paul or the other apostles as a means of persuading doubters to accept the claim that Jesus was alive - but in that case Paul could hardly have written so boldly as he did, virtually inviting anyone who wished to do so to check his story.

2. it could be said that the whole passage is a later accretion to the Corinthian letter, that Paul himself never did claim that such a large company had seen the risen Christ - but no serious scholar has any doubt that the Corinthian letter is genuine, and that our version of it is substantially the same as Paul's original letter. which leaves just one alternative:

3. there really were some 500 people still alive in Paul's day who were persuaded that they had actually seen Jesus. If they had not seen Jesus, then what did they see?

It may be possible to suggest that Jesus' close disciples were suffering from hallucinations when they claimed that he had appeared to them. But to suppose that 500 people at one time experienced an **identical** hallucination would require belief in a greater miracle psychologically than the resurrection is physically!

This whole passage, reflecting as it does the unanimous certainty of the leaders of the early church, and of a mass of ordinary Christians, that Jesus had conquered death, provides powerful and historically valid evidence that Christ truly did rise from the grave.

(4) James

This James was the half-brother of Jesus, and one of those members of Jesus' family who had thought him mad (Mk 3:21; 6:4; Jn 7:.5)[24]. He was also the author of the letter that bears his name in the NT.

What turned this former sceptical relative into a devout believer? How did James come to agree that his older brother was truly the Messiah of Israel and the eternal Son of God? Could it have been

---

[24] On the relationship between Jesus and those who are called his "brothers" and "sisters", see again your series on **Emmanuel**. On the question of whether Jesus' family thought he was "mad" (Mk 3:21), opinions differ. Some expositors think that this verse refers to friends other than his family; some think that the Greek expression most naturally refers to his family, especially since the pattern of Mark's gospel indicates that the narrative in vs 22-30 is framed between the two parallel references, vs 21 and vs 31. Vincent comments on vs 21, and the word "friends" -

"Lit. 'they whn were from beside him,' that is, by origin or birth. His mother and brethren. Compare vs 31-32. Wycliffe, 'kinsmen', Tyndale, 'they that belonged to him.' Not his disciples, since they were in the house with him." **(Word Studies In The New Testament, in loc.).**

Alford says that "friends" means "his relatives, without a doubt - for the sense is resumed in vs 31." So also Zerwick and Grosvenor (a Catholic work), Lane, and numerous others.

The matter would in any case seem to be solved by Jn 7:5, for if "his brothers did not believe in him," they could hardly have reacted in any other way to his staggering sayings about himself except to think him mentally unbalanced.

However, despite the inclusion of Mary in Mk. 3:31 (and parallels), some commentators reject the suggestion that she shared the low opinion Jesus' brothers had of him. It is pointed out that John carefully excludes Mary from his statements (7:3,5).

anything less than a shattering encounter with that same Jesus, now risen from the dead?

The way in which James became a Christian is not described in the NT, nor is his death. However, other documents fill up the gaps. For example, there is a legendary account of the conversion of James in an ancient document called **The Gospel of the Hebrews** (which was written about 100 AD). This "gospel" was quoted with respect by some of the early Fathers, and there may well be some truth in the story it tells. It seems that James was so astonished by the happenings at Calvary and the shock discovery of the empty tomb, and so appalled by his former unbelief and opposition to Jesus, that he vowed never to eat and drink again unless Jesus came back personally to forgive him -

The Lord ... went to James and appeared before him, for James had sworn that he would not eat bread ... until he saw (Jesus) raised from the dead ... The Lord said to him, 'Bring me a table and some bread' ... So he brought the bread, and (the Lord) gave thanks for it and broke it and gave it to James the Just, and said to him: 'My brother, eat your bread, for the Son of Man has risen from the dead!' "

That may be the appearance Paul had in mind when he wrote to the Corinthians. At any rate, within a few days of the resurrection (Ac 1:14), James had joined the little band of Jesus' disciples, and shortly after, he was recognised as head of the church in Jerusalem (15:13).

Paul must have heard from James himself the story of how Jesus had appeared to him (Ga 1:18-19).

Since James was the Lord's oldest brother, who had formerly thought Jesus was mad, but who was now a leading figure in the church, his testimony is singularly striking.

The strength of James' commitment to Christ as his Lord and Saviour is preserved in other traditions about his life and his martyrdom -

> "But James the brother of the Lord, who, as there were many of this name, was surnamed the Just by all ... drank neither wine nor fermented liquors, and abstained from animal food. A razor never came upon his head, he never anointed himself with oil, and never used a bath. He alone was allowed to enter the sanctuary. He never wore woollen, but linen garments. He was in the habit of entering the temple alone, and was often found upon his bended knees, and interceding for the forgiveness of the people, so that his knees became as hard as a camel's ... And indeed, on account of his exceeding great piety, he was called the Just, and Oblias ... which signifies justice and protection of the people...."

(Then follows an account of how James influenced many people to believe in Jesus. Yet at the same time, because of his diligent observance of the Jewish law, the leaders of the people failed to recognise that he was a Christian. Hence they sought his aid!)

> *" ... As there were many therefore of the rulers that believed, there arose a tumult among the Jews, Scribes, and Pharisees, saying that there was danger that the people would now expect Jesus as the Messiah. They came therefore together, and said to James, 'We entreat thee, restrain the people, who are led astray after Jesus, as if he were the Christ ... Stand therefore upon a wing of the temple, that thou mayest be conspicuous on high, and thy words may be easily heard by all the people' ...*
>
> *"The aforesaid Scribes and Pharisees therefore, placed James upon a wing of the temple, and cried out to him, 'O thou just man, whom we all ought to believe, since the people are led astray after Jesus*

that was crucified, declare to us what is the door[25] *to Jesus that was crucified.' And he answered with a loud voice, 'Why do you ask me respecting Jesus the Son of Man? He is now sitting in the heavens, on the right hand of great Power, and is about to come on the clouds of heaven!' ...*

"*(So) those same priests and Pharisees said to one another, 'We have done badly in affording such testimony to Jesus, but let us go up and cast him down, that they may dread to believe in him.' And they cried out, 'Oh, oh, Justus is himself deceived,' and they fulfilled that which is written in Isaiah, 'Let us take away the just, because he is offensive to us; wherefore they shall eat the fruit of their doings.'*

"*Going up therefore, they cast down the just man, saying to one another, 'Let us stone James the Just.' And they began to stone him, for he did not die immediately when cast down ... Thus they were stoning him, when one of the priests ... cried out, saying, 'Cease, what are you doing? Justus is praying for you!'*

"*But one of them, a fuller, beat out the brains of Justus with the club that he used to beat out clothes. Thus he suffered martyrdom, and they buried him on the spot where his tombstone is still remaining,*

---

[25] "Door" - that is, what door do we enter to learn the actual truth about Jesus. The rulers of course, expected James to expose Jesus as a charlatan.

by the temple. He became a faithful witness, both to the Jews and Greeks, that Jesus is the Christ[26]."

(5) All the Apostles

This group must be different from **"the twelve"** mentioned in verse 5. Commentators usually assume that Paul is here referring to the various appearances of Christ mentioned by Luke in Ac 1:2-3, and that **"all the apostles"** includes the people mentioned in verse 15. At any rate, this group included **"Mary his mother and his brothers"** (and presumably also his sisters, perhaps included among **"the women"**, vs 14).

Can you imagine how difficult it must have been for those members of Jesus' actual family to accept the truth about him? The gospels make it clear that they were embarrassed and angered by his public ministry and by the claims he made (see again Mt 12:46-48; 13:54-58, and note that vs 57 implies that Jesus had experienced rejection **"in his own house"**; Mk 3:21-22,31; 6:1-6; Jn 7:1-10)[27].

---

[26] That account was written by the historian Hegesippus around 150 A.D. It has been preserved for us by Eusebius, in his **Ecclesiastical History**, Bk. 2, ch. 23. Its main details are confirmed by the Jewish historian Josephus, who writes that the corrupt high priest Ananus (sic.) -

"assembled the sanhedrin of the judges, and brought before them the brother of Jesus, who was called Christ, whose name was James ... and when he had formed an accusation against (him) as a breaker of the law, he delivered (him) to be stoned."

Also records that many upright Jews were appalled at the deed, and complained to the Roman governor, who dismissed Ananus from office. The passage in Josephus was once thought to be spurious, but scholars are now inclined to believe it is basically genuine. If so, then it provides an independent witness of the martyrdom of James, dated around 93 A.D., that is, barely 30 years after James was killed. (**Antiquities of the Jews**), Bk. 20, ch. 9).

[27] However, Mary may be at least partly, if not fully, excluded from this - see again footnote (1) above.

This reaction was natural enough. It would also be natural for them to think their worst fears had been realised when he was arrested by the Jews and executed in company with common criminals. Their shame must have been bitter.

It is absurd to suppose that the horror of the **cross** could have persuaded his family to accept Jesus as their Lord! Yet within a few days of his death they **were** all thoroughly converted! And that conversion is well-attested, not only in scripture but also in other nearly contemporary documents.

It is difficult to think of anything, except the fulfilment of Jesus' own promise to rise from the dead, that could have been sufficient to persuade his mother, his brothers, and his sisters, that he was actually divine!

At least it cannot be reasonably denied that Jesus' closest relatives did come to believe he had broken the bands of death by a stupendous act of divine power, and that he had

> *"presented himself alive after his passion* by many infallible proofs*, appearing to them during forty days" (Ac 1:3).*

If that belief was a delusion, how did it arise? Why was it so convincing? What other valid reason can be offered for the conversion of these, the most unlikely converts?

(6) Paul

Last of all in this list of resurrection witnesses comes Paul, who describes himself as **"the one (who was) an abortion"** (vs 8, lit.). The phrase is emphatic in the Greek text. It carries the idea that Paul was the only one of the apostles who could be so described; and also the idea that there would never be another **"untimely"** apostle. He was the last person privileged to see with his own eyes the risen Christ in bodily form, exactly as the other apostles had seen him.

He calls himself "the abortion" because he was not even a Christian when he was confronted by the risen Christ and called to be an apostle - unlike the other apostles who had all been with Jesus

> *"from the baptism of John until the day when he was taken up" (Ac 1:22).*

Bengel says: "What 'an abortion' is among children (so Paul reckoned himself to be) among the apostles; and by this one word he sinks himself lower than in any other way. As an abortion is not worthy of the name of a man, so the apostle declares himself unworthy of the name of an apostle.[28]"

So Paul goes on to say: "**I am the least of the apostles, unfit to be called an apostle, because I persecuted the church of God.**" Yet he says that not to demean himself, but rather to magnify the graciousness of Christ. The sense is, "**even to Paul, the abortion**, Christ appeared!" (Leon Morris).

What changed this persecutor of God's church, this implacable foe, into an apostle who **"worked harder"** than any of the other apostles (vs 10)? Paul himself gives the reason in one phrase: **"Christ appeared to me!"** (cp. Ac 9:1 ff).

(II) THE EMPTY TOMB

It is sometimes suggested the apostles did not believe Jesus had actually risen bodily from the grave; that on the contrary, they used "resurrection" language merely to convey their belief that death had not been able to harm the immortal part of Christ, and that he is alive and triumphant "spiritually".

But that claim makes nonsense of the reports given in the four gospels and in Acts, which plainly describe the resurrection as a tangible and historical event. Three of the gospel writers (Matthew, Mark, and John) are listed among those who insisted they were actual eye-witnesses of the risen Christ. The other

---

[28] **New Testament Word Studies**, Kregel Publications, Grand Rapids, Michigan, 1971. Vol. 2. pg.253

gospel writer, Luke, who was also the author of Acts, specifically claims he had taken all possible care to write an orderly and historically accurate account - see Lu 1:1-4; Ac 1:1-3.

In addition, as we have seen, Paul also claims to have been an eye-witness in a special sense - Ac 9:1-6; 1 Co 15:8.

Everywhere those first disciples travelled they preached the same message - that Jesus was alive from the dead. The empty tomb was a central part of their gospel - cp Ac 2:24-32; 3:14-16,26; 4:10; 5:30; 7:55; 10:39-43. All of those references simply assume that the body of Jesus was no longer lying in Joseph's tomb.

There is no attempt to prove that assumption. It is just boldly stated, as if there could be no doubt about it. The fact is, the body was gone, and everyone knew it was gone. If there had been a body, there were plenty who would have gladly produced it! Clearly, no one could.

Where was the body? Why was it gone? The disciples, many of whom were formerly bitter enemies of Jesus (who had howled for his blood, Ac 6:7), declared there was only one possible explanation - he had risen from the dead!

All told, the NT describes at least eleven post-resurrection appearances of Christ, all of them pre-supposing that a visitor to Joseph's tomb would have found it empty. Those NT statements preclude any idea of the resurrection appearances being nothing more than immaterial visions of Christ, designed to show only that his immortal soul had survived the grave and that he was still spiritually alive.

The Christ who appeared to his disciples was no mere spectral wraith. The disciples were persuaded that they had seen the Lord himself! They had touched him! They had conversed with him! they had felt his flesh and bones! So Luke, who is acknowledged as a sober and careful historian, records that on one of the occasions when he appeared to his disciples, Jesus squashed their doubts by saying:

> "See my hands and my feet, *that it is I myself*; handle me, and see; for a spirit has not flesh and bones as you see I have" (24:39).

So it becomes impossible to deny that the disciples, and indeed everyone in Jerusalem, knew that three days after Jesus' dead body had been laid there, the tomb was empty. If Jesus did not supernaturally rise from the dead, and free himself from the tomb, then his body must have been taken by other people. But who could they have been? There are four possibilities:

(A) GRAVE ROBBERS

It has been suggested that a band of grave robbers, hearing that Jesus had been called "King of the Jews", and thinking that he might have been buried in rich garments, and with rich appurtenances, overpowered the guard of soldiers and stole the body.

What a desperate story! Even supposing it had a grain of truth, the robbers would have seen at a glance that their hopes were vain, and would have fled empty-handed. Not even the Jewish authorities were foolish enough to offer such a sorry explanation of the empty tomb.

(B) JOSEPH OF ARIMATHEA

It has been suggested that Joseph, for any one of several reasons (none of them convincing), removed the body of Jesus from the tomb, and buried it elsewhere.

But how could Joseph have done this without getting official permission to break the seals[29] and to release the body? And if he **had** gained that permission, the authorities would at once have refuted the disciples' claim that Jesus was risen.

If perchance Joseph had managed to spirit the body away before the tomb was sealed, why did he remain silent when the disciples began to claim that Jesus had risen; and who rolled away the stone?

If Joseph was himself a disciple of Jesus, he would hardly have perpetuated a lie, knowing it was bringing persecution and death upon his friends. If he was not a disciple, then he had everything to gain by advising the rulers where the body was buried, and thus incurring their favour.

(C) THE RULERS

But surely, if any of Jesus' enemies had removed his body they would have produced it as soon as the disciples began preaching the resurrection? At the very least they would have publicised the new place of burial. And why should they have removed it - especially when they had taken special care to ensure that nothing of the sort happened?

In any case, it is an historical fact that neither the Jewish nor Roman authorities ever claimed that they were the ones responsible for the empty tomb. Such a claim would have been unbelievable, and they knew it. They also knew that the tomb was empty. Where the body was they did not know, nor how Jesus had

---

[29] Mt 27:62-66; and the Gospel of Peter says: "The elders ... came to Pilate, beseeching him and saying, 'Give us soldiers, that we may guard his sepulchre for three days, lest his disciples come and steal him away, and the people suppose that he is risen from the dead and do us evil.' And Pilate gave them Petronius the centurion with soldiers to guard the tomb ... and having rolled a great stone ... they all together who were there set it at the door of the sepulchre; and they affixed seven seals, and they pitched a tent there and guarded it" (vs 29:33).

escaped from, or been taken from, the sealed tomb. So they bribed the soldiers to say that the body had been stolen by Jesus' disciples (Mt 28:11-15).

Justin Martyr (c. 100-165) indicates that this report was still being spread by the Jews in his day (**Dialogue With Trypho**, 17). And the **Gospel of Nicodemus** (c. 4th century), after describing how soldiers came to the Jewish leaders to tell them about the angel, the earthquake, the stone rolling back, and the disappearance of Jesus (cp. Mt 28:2-4), continues the story -

"At these words the Jews were afraid, and said to the soldiers: 'See that you tell this story to nobody, or all will believe in Jesus.' And for this reason they gave them also much money. And the soldiers said: 'We are afraid lest by any chance Pilate hear that we have taken money, and he will kill us.' And the Jews said: 'Take it; and we pledge ourselves that we shall speak to Pilate in your defence. Only say that you were asleep, and in your slumber the disciples came and stole him from the tomb.' The soldiers therefore took the money and said as they were bid. <u>And to this day this same lying tale is told among the Jews</u>" (Ch. 13).

(D) THE DISCIPLES

The most common suggestion, from ancient times until now, has been that the disciples stole the body of Jesus, and then pretended he had risen from the dead (cp. Mt 27:62-64). This is the most fatuous of all the attempts to explain the empty tomb. Even in Jerusalem it was not believed (cp. Ac 6:7). The disciples had nothing to gain, except torture and death, by such a fraud.

Some 1800 years ago Origen gave the obvious answer to this claim-

"A clear and unmistakable proof of the (resurrection) I hold to be the undertaking of his disciples, who devoted themselves to the teaching of a doctrine which was attended with danger to human life - a doctrine which they would not have taught with such courage had they invented the resurrection of Jesus from the dead;

and who also, at the same time, not only prepared others to despise death, but were themselves the first to manifest their disregard for its terrors" ("Against Celsus", Bk. 2, ch. 56).

The fact is, no one had any reason to remove the body from its closely sealed and guarded tomb. Unless all four gospels are rejected out of hand as fiction, without any historical value, we are left with the conclusion that Joseph's tomb was open that morning, and empty, because Jesus had truly risen from the dead.

But suppose the gospels could **not** be verified? What then? A problem still remains for the sceptic, as great as the problem of the resurrection itself -

(III) THE FIRST CHRISTIANS

There are two irreducible facts, which **are** fully verifiable historically: (a) the unshakeable **belief** of Christians from the very beginning that Jesus had literally walked out of the grave; and (b) the existence of a **church** built on that belief.

Apart from the resurrection, how are those two things to be explained?

If Jesus did not rise, why were so many people so convinced he had risen they gladly sacrificed everything they possessed rather than surrender that conviction? If Jesus did not rise, how can the church be accounted for? What turned that group of shattered, terrified people into towering prophets of God, utterly fearless, stunning in spiritual authority and in the power of their witness? What turned their grief into gladness, their timidity into toughness, their confusion into confidence, their fear into faith?

Those early Christians had no doubt about the answer to such questions: **it was the resurrection**, of which they claimed to have been eye-witnesses. No other satisfactory explanation has ever been offered.

But then, almost from the day of Pentecost, the church began to point, not so much to the appearances of Christ, nor even to the empty tomb, but rather to **itself** as the chief proof of the resurrection. If Christ had not risen, how could observers explain the existence of the **church**? How could they explain the marvellous things that were daily happening among the Christians? To those first disciples, the living **church** was undeniable evidence of a living **Christ**.

So Peter, already on the day of Pentecost, pointed to the outpouring of the Spirit as proof that Jesus was alive (Ac 2:33) - and from that time on, every new miracle, every new act of grace, confirmed the message of the empty tomb: **Christ is alive!**

Surprisingly, all of this is confirmed by the incomplete and divergent accounts contained in the four gospels. They do not attempt to give formal documentary proof of the resurrection. The people for whom the gospels were written were in the main already convinced that Jesus was alive. They had seen all the proof they needed of that fact, both in the church and in their own lives. The resurrection accounts in the gospels were adequate to satisfy the special purposes of each writer - thus, for example, Matthew was particularly concerned with the manner in which Jesus fulfilled OT prophecy, especially in the Galilean ministry, so he emphasises the Galilean appearances of the risen Christ (4:12-16; 28:7,10,16-20).

No one has ever claimed that those accounts by themselves are adequate to prove the resurrection beyond all doubt. If the gospel writers had intended their reports to be taken as formal proof of the resurrection they would have been careful to record each appearance of Christ in proper sequence, with details of the witnesses, and these accounts would have been given much more space than they presently have.

As it is, the accounts are brief, they differ considerably from each other, and it is plain that the writers did not feel obliged to set down everything they knew about the various appearances of Christ. They were content to write only as much as suited their purpose.

The fact is, all the teachers in the early church knew that only one thing could possibly prove that the resurrection of Jesus was not a fake: namely, **evidence of his grace and power at work each day in the church.**

The same proof is still the most valid today. If the resurrection were nothing more than an historical event it would long ago have lost interest for everyone but historians. But our cry is not, **"Christ arose!"** Rather, it is **"CHRIST IS ALIVE!"**

Nothing could be more pathetic than a church in which the resurrection has become only an ancient memory. We need to show by his continuing activity among us that Christ is alive today, unchanged in power, still confirming his word with signs, wonders, and miracles!

It should be remembered that for the first few decades of Christian history the church itself was the only proof that Jesus was alive from the dead. Those first Christians lacked any written New Testament, and were dependent for their faith entirely upon their preachers, and upon God bearing those preachers witness by the power of the Holy Spirit (He 2:4). If the NT had never been written that witness would have remained valid, and remains valid today, so long as the church is still flourishing as the Spirit-filled "body" of her living Head.

Linked with the church there are three other factors for which the resurrection alone seems to be an adequate explanation -

(A) THE NEW TESTAMENT

"If Jesus had not risen, the New Testament would never have been written. For who would take the trouble to write the biography of anyone who had laid tremendous claims to Messiahship and divinity, but whose career terminated in a shameful death? But (God be praised) Jesus did arise, and that is why the group of men who wrote the books of the New Testament took up their pens with such enthusiasm and holy conviction[30]."

There is an extraordinary thing about the gospel writers. Their accounts of the resurrection of Jesus introduced an astonishing new order of being, one for which there was no precedent either in Jewish or pagan writings.

They had two models they could have chosen. One, the Jewish, thought of the resurrection of the dead as essentially a resuscitation of the original body; certainly changed and made more beautiful, but still physical, sensuous, and not greatly changed from its former nature (rather like the Muslim view - see chapter Seven in this series).

The other model, the Greek, argued that the only possible kind of resurrection (even if there were such a thing) would be altogether spiritual, non-corporeal, one in which the soul would be completely emancipated from the body.

The gospel writers, with remarkable boldness (unless of course they were telling the simple truth), combined both models, and thus created an order of being that had never before been imagined.

That fact is so striking, it has compelled the critics to argue, either that the **spiritual** elements of the story were added to what was actually just a recovery from unconsciousness; or the exact reverse, that the **bodily** elements of the story were added to what were actually just spiritual visions!

Contrary to the critics, we may confidently say that "the marvel of the (gospels) is the perfect simplicity, the perfect naturalness, with which the two sets of characteristics are combined in the same narratives,'as if those who put the facts together were conscious of no difficulty in the apparent contradiction' (**Westcott**). If we take

---

[30] Norval Geldenhuys, in his fine commentary on the Gospel of Luke, in The New International Commentary on the New Testament, Eerdmans Publishing Co., Michigan, 1977 printing, pg. 628.

one series of events, the resurrection might appear to have been a mere coming back to life; if we take another, it might appear to be purely spiritual ... But the records combine both, and thus differentiate the apostolic representation of the resurrection of Jesus from the two current conceptions - from the sensuous conception of it held by the Pharisees, and from the spiritualistic concept of the Alexandrians, or the Greek philosophers".[31]

(B) THE OBSERVANCE OF SUNDAY

"The fact that the Christian church from an early date has observed Sunday instead of Saturday as the day of rest, can only be explained from the fact of the resurrection of Jesus on the Sunday morning (cp. Ac 20:7; 1 Co 16:2; Re 1:10; and cp. also references in the Fathers from as early as the first century) ... And if we bear in mind that the first congregations consisted mainly of converted Jews (who were firmly attached to Saturday as the Sabbath) and that the leaders of the church were men like Paul who had had a strict training according to the Law, then only the fact that Jesus arose on a Sunday ... can explain why the old Jewish custom was given up and the first day of the week accepted as the day of rest...[32]"

(C) THE EUCHARIST

Christian Communion, or the observance of the Lord's Supper, has from the very beginning of the church been called the **eucharist**, which means, **the thanksgiving**. Yet the observance itself is a commemoration of **death**, using the seemingly gruesome symbols of bread representing human flesh, and wine representing human blood. The death remembered is that of Christ.

Why should those first disciples have wanted to remind themselves continually of the horror of Calvary, which killed their Lord; and

---

[31] Hastings Dictionary of the Bible, Vol 4; pg 346; 1973 reprint by Baker Book House, Ann Arbor, Michigan.

[32] Ibid. pg. 629.

even more, why should they do so with gladness and gratitude? Yet, apparently against all reason, that is just what they did do. See Ac 2:46-47; 20:7; 1 Co 10:16-17, 20-21; 11:20-34; and the following -

"Now concerning the Thanksgiving (Eucharist), thus give thanks. First, concerning the cup: We thank thee, our Father, for the holy vine of David thy servant, which thou madest known to us through Jesus they servant; to thee be the glory for ever. And concerning the broken bread: We thank thee, our Father, for the life and knowledge which thou madest known to us through Jesus thy servant; to thee be the glory for ever ... for thine is the glory and the power through Jesus Christ for ever" (**The Teaching of the Twelve Apostles**, c. 100 A.D.).

"On the day of the resurrection of the Lord, that is, the Lord's day, assemble yourselves together, without fail, giving thanks to God, and praising him for those mercies God has bestowed upon you through Christ ... that your sacrifice may be unspotted, and acceptable to God ... Be ye always thankful, as faithful and honest servants; and concerning the eucharistical thanksgiving say thus: We thank thee, our Father, for that life which thou hast made known to us by Jesus thy Son" ... (**Constitutions of the Holy Apostles**, Bk. 7, Sec. 2, ch. 25,30; c. 4th century).

Here then is an arresting fact: the death of Jesus celebrated with joy as a regular part of the worship of the early church. What can explain this seemingly bizarre development? Nothing seems adequate except the explanation the Christians themselves gave: **the crucifixion was followed by the resurrection, which turned unspeakable tragedy into limitless triumph!**

CHAPTER SIX:

THE EMPTY TOMB

In this chapter we begin an examination of the arguments people use, who refuse to believe that Jesus actually did rise bodily from the dead.

(I) AGAINST THE RESURRECTION

We have already looked at one theory, that the body of Jesus was removed by the Jews, or by the disciples, or by someone else. That theory was shown to be improbable. However, there are a number of other objections that have been raised against the resurrection[33] -

(A) MIRACLES DON'T HAPPEN

In the end, every argument against the Easter event arises from a basic premise that the miracle of the resurrection is impossible - it simply could not have happened. To people who reject the very idea of a miracle, almost any explanation of the empty tomb is more acceptable than the supernatural one offered in the gospels.

There is no doubt that the basic problem connected with the resurrection has always been the staggering miracle involved. Even ancient peoples, who may have been deeply superstitious and credulous in other matters, reeled back from the claim that Jesus had risen from the dead (cp. Ac 18:32). It has always been easier for some people to believe that the witnesses were liars, or mistaken, than to believe, against universal experience, that a man has broken the chains of death.

---

[33] Some of these arguments, and related matters, are discussed in the VCC series on When The Trumpet Sounds, and also in the series The Authority of the Bible.

At the open mouth of Joseph's new garden tomb, two opposing world-views confront each other. The missing body of Jesus is the great divide. Only two explanations are possible: **either God performed the most astonishing miracle ever recorded; or the mystery must be solved within ordinary natural limits.** In the end, people accept or reject the resurrection for reasons that are not historical, but are based rather on their existing view of life and of the world around them.

Thus there are some who could not accept that Jesus rose from the dead without first changing the naturalistic pre-suppositions that dominate their outlook. Even if every difficulty could be removed from the gospel accounts, and the historicity of the event made undeniable, they would still refuse to believe that such a supernatural happening was possible. For them, miracles simply do not happen.

Sadly, that naturalism has invaded the church, so that those modern preachers who want to maintain credibility with the world, offer all kinds of theories about what they reckon was the real nature of the resurrection. They struggle to keep the **benefits** of the doctrine that Jesus lives, yet they want to deny the **fact** upon which that doctrine is built.

But that will not do. It is like trying to keep the savour of an orange while banning all oranges. Or, perhaps better, to keep on being fed by bread that one refuses to eat!

Yet miracles become difficult to accept only on a view that the physical universe is a closed system, self-supporting, running with universal conformity, according to immutable laws. Is that a reasonable view?

(1) Can Miracles Happen?

The idea that our world exists in a secure and static environment, without any possibility of supernatural or divine intervention, may be acceptable to atheists (although it cannot conceivably be "proved", and must depend on an act of faith), but it should certainly not have a place in the thinking of any person who acknowledges God. It is also a view toward which the Bible is utterly antagonistic. Everywhere, scripture insists that God is imminent in the world he has made. He cannot be removed from it. Jesus himself affirmed, **"My Father is working still, and I am working!"** (Jn 5:17) - that is, God is dynamically active in the world, and continually involved in human affairs.

From the standpoint of scripture, then, there is then no real distinction between "natural" and "supernatural" - except that the former represents the way things normally happen on earth, whereas the latter represents a rarer pattern of divine action.

(2) Saint Augustine of Hippo

Augustine commented on this issue long ago:

> *"... how can an event be contrary to nature when it happens by the will of God, since the will of the great Creator assuredly is the nature of every created thing? A portent, therefore, does not occur contrary to nature, but contrary (only to what is presently) known of nature ... Then why should not God have power to make the bodies of the dead rise again ... since he made the world so full of innumerable marvels in the sky, on the earth, in the air, and in the water - although the world itself is beyond doubt a marvel greater and more wonderful than all the wonders with which it is filled? ... For when they refuse to believe something, alleging its impossibility, and demand that we supply a rational explanation, we reply that the explanation is the will of Almighty God. For God is certainly called 'Almighty' for one reason only (because) he has the power to do whatever he wills, and he has the power to create so many things which would be reckoned obviously impossible, if they were not displayed to our senses or else reported by*

> *witnesses who have always proved reliable ... And yet the natural phenomena known to all men are no less wonderful, and would be a source of astonishment to all who observe them, if it were not man's habit to restrict his wonder at miracles to the rarities[34] ..."*

Are we going to assume that the so-called laws of nature are their own source, and their own reason for existence, that they represent ultimate truth, and beyond them there can be no knowledge? Even those who do assume this (and it has to be an assumption, for there is no way of "proving" it) give the lie to their own belief; for every hour of every day, when they recognise such intangibles as love, joy, beauty, virtue, they proclaim the existence of things that no mere natural law can explain.

We cannot be imprisoned within such a narrow purview. We insist that the laws of nature are nothing more than a means, to an end that transcends nature and finds its goal in God.

But as soon as that is accepted, miracles no longer become impossible, nor even improbable. No act of God, no matter how unusual, can be said to violate some "inviolable" law, for the only such law is the will of God himself!

(3) The Witness of Mankind

Consider the emergence of man himself (whether by evolutionary processes or by fiat of God makes no difference in this place): man represents the introduction into the world of a species dramatically different from any other on earth. His capabilities and nature, from the point of view of other creatures, are unimaginable, and would certainly seem to them to be supernatural. The coming of man upon the earth introduced new powers, new achievements that, in contrast with all that had gone

---

[34] **City of God**, tr. by Henry Bettenson; ed. by David Knowles; Penguin Books, London, 1972; pg. 976, 977, 980, 981.

before, were scarcely less remarkable than the new things introduced by the coming of Christ.

If Jesus truly did represent a **"new Adam"** (as scripture says), then it is not surprising that new happenings were associated with his coming, culminating in his resurrection. And while it may be difficult to conceive of an ordinary man, already dying because of sin, being able to raise himself from the dead, why should it be thought improbable that the unique Christ, free from all corruption, should be able to do so? (cp. Ac 2:27).

At least, Jesus was a man so **"separate from sinners"** that no-one can say with certainty what was possible or impossible for him (except that he could not do anything inconsonant with his real humanity).

(4) Not In A Vacuum

Again, although the resurrection was a unique event, it certainly did not occur in isolation, or without prior indications. Rather, scripture describes it as an inevitable climax to the succession of equally astonishing happenings that surrounded the birth and life of Jesus.

Yet even those events did not spring un-announced onto the pages of history, but were themselves the result of an unbroken line of divine action, beginning way back in the Garden of Eden!

So from this perspective the resurrection ceases to be an invasion of the abnormal into the normal, but becomes rather the **necessary culmination** of a divine involvement in human affairs that has been continuous with human history. The resurrection was not a violation of natural law, but was in fact quite congruous with God's unchanging manner of working in the world.

In view of all the available evidence, it is easier, and I would say more rational, to accept the scriptural view of life than to accept the opposite view, of the world as a closed system, governed solely by physical laws, with God, if he exists, quite absent from it.

(5) A Faith-choice

Eventually, each person has to make his own choice, which is essentially a step beyond the evidence. He may use his reason to bring him to the brink, but the chasm itself must be crossed by a leap of faith. All who make this leap toward God find that their faith becomes **self-authenticating**; or, to use the more pungent language of scripture:

> *"If we receive the testimony of men, the testimony of God is greater; for this is the testimony of God that he has borne witness to his Son. He who believes in the Son of God has the testimony in himself. He who does not believe God has made him a liar, because he has not believed in the testimony that God has borne of his Son" (1 Jn 5:9-11).*

(B) JESUS DID NOT DIE ON THE CROSS

"(Another) implausible effort to explain the rise of the resurrection faith is the 'swoon theory'' ... (which explains) the 'resurrection' of Jesus in terms of his non-death.

> *(This theory claims) that crucifixion was usually a slow, protracted dying, and cases are on record of victims who were crucified, taken down from the cross alive, and survived. Jesus 'died' in an amazingly short time. The loud cry he uttered shortly before his 'death' shows that his strength was far from exhausted. His 'death' was only a death-like trance. The thrust of the spear in Jesus' side was no more than a surface wound. However, Jesus appeared to have expired and so was taken down from the cross and laid in the tomb. The cool grave and the aromatic spices contributed to the process of resuscitation, and finally the storm and the earthquake roused Jesus to full consciousness. The earthquake also had the effect of rolling the stone away from the entrance to the tomb. Jesus*

> *stripped off the grave clothes, and put on a gardener's outfit he managed to procure. That is why Mary mistook him for the gardener (Jn 20:15)".*[35]

(1) Stretching Credulity

If that theory were true, then we would have to believe one of three things:

1. when the disciples found that Jesus was still alive they agreed to conspire with him in pretending he had actually risen from the dead; or

2. despite his terrible wounds, and being weak from loss of blood, fainting, barely half-alive, Jesus performed the astonishing "miracle" of persuading his disciples that he had actually been raised from the dead; or

3. having escaped from the tomb, Jesus then went into hiding, and in due course died, without even his closest friends knowing he had died, so that they were left to believe he had risen.

Any one of those conclusions demands more credulity than is required to believe in the resurrection! Such arguments stubbornly refuse to face all of the evidence contained in scripture and history; they choose those pieces of evidence that seem to fit the theory, and ignore the remainder. It would seem more honest to reject the four gospels outright, allowing them no credibility. But if the gospels are allowed to speak at all, then there are some parts of their witness that cannot be rationally denied; and on one thing they are forcibly unanimous: **Jesus really died**.

Thus Mark writes:

---

[35] Ladd, op. cit., pg. 134. Note that Ladd calls this theory "implausible".

> "Jesus uttered a loud cry, and breathed his last ... (and) Joseph of Arimathea ... took courage and went to Pilate, and asked for the body of Jesus. And Pilate wondered if he were already dead; and summoning the centurion, he asked him whether he was already dead. And when he learned from the centurion that he was dead, he granted the body to Joseph" *(15:39-45; and cp. also the other three gospels).*

It would perhaps not be difficult for me to assume mistakenly that a man was dead - I have had little contact with death - but a Roman centurion would hardly be so easily duped. I am as willing to accept his word on the matter as Pilate was. The centurion was emphatic: "**He is dead!**"

(2) Origen's Reply To Celsus

When Celsus accused Jesus of faking his death, and of pretending to rise again, like some mythical Greek hero, Origen replied:

> *"Let us endeavour to show that the account of Jesus being raised from the dead cannot possibly be compared to these. For each one of the heroes ... (may indeed) have secretly withdrawn himself from the sight of men, and returned again, if so determined, to those whom he had left; but seeing that Jesus was crucified before all the Jews, and his body slain in the presence of his nation, how can they bring themselves to say that he practised a similar deception as those (mythical) heroes ... (Now) if we were to suppose Jesus to have died an obscure death, so that the fact of his decease was not patent to the whole nation of the Jews ... there would in such a case have been ground for the same suspicion entertained regarding the heroes being also entertained regarding himself (that he did not really die).*

> *Probably, then, in addition to other causes for the crucifixion of Jesus, this also may have contributed to his dying a conspicuous death upon the cross, that no one might have it in his power to say that he voluntarily withdrew from the sight of men and seemed only to die, without really doing so; but, appearing again, made a juggler's trick of the resurrection from the dead[36]."*

(3) Saint John Chrysostom

Chrysostom (c 380), in one of his majestic homilies on the resurrection, took equal care to show that Jesus had died:

> *" ... it was providentially ordered that the body of Jesus should be placed in a new tomb, wherein no one had been placed before. This prevented anyone from claiming that it was not Jesus who rose, but another who lay there with him. It also enabled the disciples to come easily, and watch the burial of Jesus, because the place was near. Nor were they the only witnesses of his burial; his enemies also, by placing seals on the tomb, and by setting soldiers to watch over it, behaved like men testifying that they were performing a burial. For Christ earnestly desired that his burial should be confessed, no less than his resurrection. Therefore, the disciples were very earnest about showing that he truly died. All succeeding time would suffice to confirm the resurrection; but if at that time his death had been partially concealed, or was made in some way doubtful, then this would likely have harmed the first account of the resurrection. Nor was it only for these reasons that he was publicly buried, but also*

---

[36] Against Celsus, Bk. 2, ch. 56

> *that the story about stealing his body might be proved false" (Homily #85, On St John).*

In the same manner, Paul emphasises the fact that Jesus not only "**died**", but that he was also "**buried**" (1 Co 15:3-4). To say he was "**buried**" seems superfluous. Why not just say, "**he died for our sins, and he was raised on the third day**"? Why say, "**he died, he was buried, he was raised**"? And why stress that his burial was one of those matters of "**first importance**" that Paul had "**received**", and that he had taken many pains to "**deliver**" to the Corinthians?

Paul does elsewhere ascribe a theological significance to the burial of Christ (cp. Ro 6:4; Cl 1:12), but here his main concern seems to be an emphatic declaration that Jesus **died bodily**, was **buried bodily**, and **rose bodily** - thus preventing any claim either that Jesus did not truly die or was not truly raised.

Chrysostom, later in the same homily, argues further against the possibility that the body was stolen:

> *" ... (Peter and John) drew near with great eagerness to the sepulchre, and they saw the linen cloths lying there, which was a sign of the resurrection. For, if any persons had removed the body, they would not have stripped it before doing so; nor, if any had stolen it, would they have taken the trouble to remove the head cloth, and roll it up, and lay it in a place by itself. What would they have done? They would have taken the body as it was. On this account, John tells us by anticipation that it was buried with much myrrh, which glues to the body no less firmly than lead, so that when you hear that the head cloth lay apart, you will not endure those who say that he was stolen. A thief would not have been so foolish as to spend so much trouble on a superfluous matter. For why should he unwrap*

> *the cloths? And how could he have escaped detection if he had done so ... ?"*

Chrysostom continues with this argument, and he shows how careful the disciples were to establish that while the body was missing, the wrapping cloths were lying apparently undisturbed - a situation impossible for thieves to achieve. All of this, he says, is written so that we might believe in the resurrection. The homily concludes with a remarkable and pungent censure of elaborate funerals, based on the fact that Jesus rose naked from the dead![37]

Jesus of Nazareth was put to death by Pontius Pilate. In all history there is no fact more certain than that; except perhaps that three days later he broke loose from the tomb, to live for evermore!

(C) THE RESURRECTION APPEARANCES WERE HALLUCINATIONS

(1) An Ancient Argument

One of the oldest and most persistent arguments against the resurrection is that the appearances of the risen Christ were actually hallucinations. It is argued that the disciples, mentally distraught at the death of their beloved Friend, and yearning to see him again, were ripe subjects for mental delusion.

This self-deception, it is said, began with the women who became convinced they had met the risen Jesus near the garden tomb. They may have confused a gardener with Jesus. Or, in their excited state of mind, they may have imagined the form of Jesus veiled in the morning mist. Or they might even have conjured up a phantasm of Jesus by their own distraught imaginations.

At any rate, what they saw was an apparition, after the fashion of the ghosts and other spirit-beings people today sometimes claim they have seen. Nonetheless, the women were so convinced they truly **had** seen Jesus, and that he was alive, and their joy was so

---

[37] See Lesson Four, footnote 5.

contagious, the other disciples were themselves caught up in this belief and they also began to "see" Jesus.

(2) The Witnesses Were Few

The proponents of this argument claim it is re-enforced by the fact that no one other than the disciples "saw" Jesus; but if he were really alive, they say, it is inconceivable that he would not have shown himself more widely.

It is true, the contagious joy of those who had seen Jesus did communicate itself to the other disciples, and it certainly did create in them a hope that they might also be privileged to see the Lord. But to attribute to hallucinations the joyful testimony of the first witnesses, and the subsequent encounters with Christ experienced by the other disciples, stretches credulity beyond reason. Consider the following -

(a) I have already offered an explanation (in Chapter Four) of why Jesus appeared only to his disciples, and even to them only in a limited manner. Notice also that Jesus himself declared that those who did not want to believe would not believe, even if a man were to be raised from the dead (Lu 16:31). Then there was the occasion when his brothers, who did not yet believe in him, demanded that he stop working in secret, and that he show himself openly to the world. But Jesus declined to do so. He insisted the time would come when he would irresistibly reveal himself to the whole world. But until then, eyes to see him would be given only to those who are willing to see him (Jn 7:3-5; and cp. Mt 26:63-65).

(b) The women went to the cemetery early on Sunday morning, not looking for an empty grave, but to anoint a dead body. The main thing on their minds was not an expectation that they might encounter a miracle, but rather, how they could roll aside the heavy stone (Mk 16:1-3). Hallucinations normally occur when one is expecting or wanting them to occur. There is no evidence that either the women, or any of the disciples, were expecting that Jesus would rise from the dead. In fact, all of the available evidence suggests that such an idea never entered their heads: Mt 28:17; Mk 16:8, 11, 14; Lu 24:11, 25, 37; Jn 20:24, 25.

(c) Hallucinations are normally individual. Even if hallucinatory expectations are passed from one person to another, so that they "see" similar apparitions, it is unknown for a motley group of people, who are not expecting to see anything, instantaneously to see the same apparition. It would be very unusual even for two people to experience an identical hallucination, though they are close together, and both undergoing the same psychological pressures. Yet different people, in isolated places, at quite different times, all saw the same risen Christ.

(The cavil that women were the first witnesses of the risen Christ - with its implied slur that they were prone to hysteria, and therefore unreliable - was probably an early complaint against the resurrection. This may be the reason why Paul omitted the two Marys from his list of witnesses in 1 Co 15:1-7. Not that he doubted the testimony of the women, but he may have been trying to avoid giving anyone even slight grounds upon which to question the reliability of the witnesses.)

(d) Why did those "hallucinations" suddenly cease? If the risen Christ were only a phantom it would have been more natural for sightings of him to increase in frequency, not to end so unexpectedly and dramatically (Ac 1:9). Yet Paul had no hesitation in saying that he had witnessed the final resurrection appearances of Christ (1 Co 15:8-9). There would be no more such appearances. If Christ is seen again, it actually will be a visionary experience, quite different in character to the resurrection appearances.

(e) Note that "a vision of departed persons does not necessarily imply their resurrection. When Moses and Elijah were seen at the Transfiguration of Christ, did the disciples infer their resurrection? Contemporary belief in the Apostolic age had assumed that patriarch and prophet and saint of OT times lived on in Paradise, but this did not involve belief in their resurrection. Visions were perfectly compatible with the continuance of a dead body in the grave, and no belief in its resurrection would ensue. Why then did the Apostle, having seen Christ after his death, affirm his resurrection? Was it not because this 'seeing' of him was consciously different from the seeing in a dream, or from any kind of seeing, except one involving physical identity?"[38]

(D) THE WRONG TOMB

This theory argues that in the morning dusk the women, being strangers to Jerusalem, went to a tomb they mistakenly thought was the place where Jesus was buried. They were astonished to find the grave open, but a young man, who was working in the entrance to the tomb, guessed their purpose, and tried to show them where Jesus was actually buried: "He is not here," he began to say, "come and see the place where they laid him" - and he probably began to walk toward a nearby burying place. But the nervous and overwrought women imagined they had met an angel and fled in terror, thinking also that Jesus had risen.

That ingenious argument is based on a convenient omission of the words, "He is risen!" which were spoken by the young man (or the angel, as the case may be), and it also gives a sense to his other words that the gospel writers never thought of (Mt 28:5-7; Mk 16:5-7; Lu 24:1-7).

It is improbable that the women could have been so mistaken, for they had taken careful note of where Jesus was buried (Mk 15:47; Lu 23:55). In any case, when the women reported what they had seen, Peter and John ran to the garden to inspect the tomb themselves. They too found it empty, but with the linen burial cloths still lying in place. There can be no doubt that Jesus' body was missing. Yet the theory assumes that the body was still in the "right" tomb. That is contrary to all the evidence.

---

[38] W. S. Simpson, in Hastings Dictionary of the New Testament, Vol 2; Baker Book House, Michigan; 1973 reprint; pg 511.

The unassailable fact that the body of Jesus was no longer in the grave brings all of the various explanations of the resurrection to grief. If the disciples had in fact looked into the wrong tomb, how easily it would have been for the Jewish authorities to silence their preaching of the resurrection simply by producing the corpse. That they failed to do so, and failed also to give an adequate explanation of the missing body, becomes itself a silent witness to the resurrection.

As James Orr once wrote: "The empty tomb remains an unimpeachable witness to the truth of the message that the Lord has risen."

(E) A DELIBERATE FABRICATION

It has often been suggested, either that Jesus himself fabricated his "resurrection" (by anticipating his quick removal from the cross and resuscitation in the tomb), or that the resurrection was a fiction promulgated by the disciples in order to take advantage of the thousands of people who revered Jesus as a prophet.

We reply

1. the character of Christ hardly fits that of a schemer and fraud, a religious faker.
2. there were too many disparate witnesses to the resurrection to make it credible that they were all part of an unscrupulous plot.
3. those witnesses were basically people of upright character, who themselves, in the name of Jesus, preached morality, integrity, honesty; they were hardly the kind of people who would knowingly proclaim a lie.
4. those early disciples were willing to die horribly rather than deny this "fabrication" - a fact of history that defies normal experience even more than the resurrection may seem to do.

5. it is impossible that such disorganised and frightened men as the disciples were after Jesus' death could have organised such an elaborate scheme overnight - as they would have had to do, because they were not expecting Jesus' sudden arrest and execution.

6. if the resurrection story is fiction, why did the gospel writers not collaborate to produce identical versions of it (which would have enhanced its veracity), and why did they not build into the story at least one person who actually saw Jesus rise from the dead?

Here is an astonishing fact: the story bears none of the marks of fiction, but all the marks of an event so profoundly believed that none of the writers felt it necessary to describe the event in detailed sequence. They merely selected what was pertinent to their own message, and they differed from each other because of the different way in which each of them recalled those stunning hours, and the different effect an encounter with the risen Christ had had on each of them.

The restraint, the sobriety, the sense of factuality in the canonical gospels stands in sharp contrast to the exaggerated fictions of the various apocryphal gospels (which do attempt, vainly, to give a detailed account of the resurrection, with many additional, but probably fictitious, witnesses) [39].

Then we may ask, lastly, what did they do with the body? Was it buried? cast into the ocean? burned to ashes? And if so, who did it? How was the secret kept so well, even when friends and family of the perpetrators began to be imprisoned and murdered for proclaiming that Christ is alive?

In the end, the only sensible explanation of the empty tomb, is the one given in the gospels: the third day after he was buried, Jesus was somehow raised from the dead. The gospels attribute that act to the power of God; and they see in it an event utterly unique in history, the source of our own marvellous victory over the grave.

---

[39] The Gospel of Peter (c.150) is a good example of the things a fictional gospel might add to the canonical gospels. Note especially verse 10, also the claim that the soldiers actually saw Jesus come out of the tomb.

(8) " ... early in the morning as the sabbath was drawing on, there came a multitude from Jerusalem and the region round about, that they might see the sepulchre that was sealed. (9) And in the night in which the Lord's day was drawing on, as the soldiers kept guard two by two in a watch, there was a great voice in heaven; and they saw the heavens opened, and two men descended from thence with great light and approached the tomb. And that stone which was put at the door rolled of itself and made way in part; and the tomb was opened, and both the young men entered in. (10) When therefore those soldiers saw it, they wakened the centurion and the elders; for they too were hard by, keeping guard. And, as they declared what things they had seen, again they see three men come forth from the tomb, and two of them supporting one, and a cross following them; and of the two the head reached unto the heaven, but the head of him that was led by them overpassed the heavens. And they heard a voice from the heavens, saying, Thou hast preached to them that sleep. And a response was heard from the cross, Yea. (11) They therefore ... hastened in the night to Pilate ... and declared all things which they had seen, being greatly distressed and saying, Truly he was the Son of God. Pilate answered and said, I am pure from the blood of the Son of God ..."

(F) THEY SAW A SPIRIT

Some critics try to retain the values of the resurrection, but to escape the presumed embarrassment of claiming that a dead man actually came to life again, by suggesting that the resurrection appearances were spiritual, not physical, in nature. The disciples (they say) saw visions of Jesus in his familiar form. Those visions were not hallucinatory spectres, but supernatural revelations of the glorified Christ. His dead body, now discarded, still lay in the tomb, but the living spirit of Christ having returned to heaven, and being enthroned at the Father's right hand, was shown to the disciples. These spiritual visions of Christ were given to the disciples by God to assure them that death had not destroyed him, and that they too would one day conquer the grave.

Four objections to that theory have been raised -

(1) If the risen Christ appeared to be real, and claimed that he was real (Lu 24:39), yet all the time he was not real, then he was guilty of an extraordinary deception. We might well ask, Why? What useful purpose could be served by giving the disciples a false impression? It is claimed that the fault was in the disciples, who misinterpreted what they saw, we ask again, Why then didn't Christ correct them when he saw that they were mistaken? On the contrary, he continued to speak and behave exactly like a man risen from the dead, and not at all like a mere spirit who lacked real substance.

(2) The theory fails at the very point it seeks to avoid: a supernatural occurrence. It replaces the real miracle of the bodily resurrection of Jesus by the pseudo-miracle of a spiritual manifestation. But if people cannot accept the real miracle (because they refuse to accept anything supernatural), then they will hardly be likely to accept this pale replacement. It adds nothing of value to what scripture reveals, yet strips the resurrection of the main part of its drama and power.

(3) All the gospel evidence shows that the risen Christ was in some way still physical. He ate, he drank, he spoke, he was substantial - Lu 24:36-43; Jn 20:17-18; 21:9 ff.

(4) The theory leaves unsolved the problem of the empty tomb. If the disciples saw anything at all they saw a real man. If that is not accepted, then one may as well discard the NT, for the whole book is built upon the premise that "the same Jesus" the disciples had known and loved, whom they had placed in the tomb, had risen from the dead and shown himself alive to them by "many infallible proofs" (Ac 1:3, 11).

If that testimony is not trustworthy, there is simply no point in trying to salvage anything from it, for the Christian gospel would then have a lie at its very heart. If the gospels are the writings of honest witnesses, then there is no room to suggest that the appearances of the risen Christ were either subjective visions, conjured up in the minds of hysterical disciples, nor objective visions sent to the disciples by God.

In other words, the resurrection appearances were what the gospels claim them to have been: **the words and actions of the only Man in history who has ever mastered death.**

(II) WHO RAISED CHRIST FROM THE DEAD?

Here is an interesting question: did Jesus rise or was he raised from the dead? That is, did he conquer death by his own unaided power, or was his resurrection an act of the Father?

Both ideas are taught in the NT.

There are places that indicate the resurrection was an act of Christ: Jn 10:18 (where he claims power to raise himself); and the following (where he is described as "rising" from the dead, not as "being raised"), Mk 8:31; 9:9; 10:34; Ac 17:3; 1 Th 4:14; etc. And there are places that indicate the resurrection was an act of the Father: Ro 4:24; 6:4; 1 Co 15:15; Ga 1:1; etc.

It is evident, then, that the resurrection was a joint act by both the Father and the Son. Insofar as Jesus was a man, and a son who was perfected by his obedience, it was fitting that the Father should vindicate his righteous Servant by raising him from the dead. It was not possible that the Father should permit his Holy One to face corruption in the grave (Ac 2:27).

But insofar as Jesus was also the eternal Logos, it was fitting that he should exercise his divine prerogative to master death by an act of his own power. He could have been raised by the Father's hand alone; he could have raised himself by his own hand alone; but it suited the wider purposes of God that Father and Son should act jointly in performing this stupendous miracle.

The third Person of the Godhead, the Holy Spirit, was also deeply involved in this immense task, as suggested in He 9:14; 1 Pe 3:18).

On Jn 10:18, Barnes writes:

> *"(Jesus said), 'No man taketh my life from me.' That is, 'no one can take it by force, or unless I am willing to yield myself into their hands.'*
>
> *He had power to preserve his life, as he showed by so often escaping from the Pharisees; he voluntarily went up to Jerusalem, knowing he would die; he knew the approach of Judas to betray him; and he expressly told Pilate at his bar that he could have no power at all against him, except it were given him, by his Father (Jn 19:11).*
>
> *"Jesus had a right to lay down his life for the good of men. The patriot dies for his country on the field of battle; the merchant exposes his life for gain; and the Son of God had a right to put himself in the way of danger and of death, when his church and the dying world needed such an atoning sacrifice.*
>
> *"This shows the peculiar love of Jesus. His death was voluntary. His coming was voluntary - the fruit*

*of love. His death was the fruit of love. He was permitted to choose the **time** and **mode** of his death. He did. He chose the most painful, lingering, ignominious manner of death then known to man, and thus showed his love.*

"Then he said, 'I have power ... to take it again.' This shows that he was Divine. A dead man has no power to raise himself from the grave. And as Jesus had this power after he was deceased, it proves that there was some other nature than that which expired, to which the term 'I' might be still applied. None but God can raise the dead; and as Jesus had this power over his own body, it proves that he was Divine[40]."

---

[40] **Notes on the New Testament**, in loc.; Kregel Publications, Grand Rapids, Michigan; 1962 reprint.

CHAPTER SEVEN:

AN IMMORTAL SOUL?

Many phenomenal results are associated with the resurrection of Christ. All of these but one will be considered in the next chapter. The one exception is the most obvious benefit we gain from the empty tomb: a guarantee that since Jesus lives, we shall live also. One day our graves will be as empty as his. Because he rose, we too shall rise, and for us death has been forever defeated.

(I) INTIMATIONS OF IMMORTALITY

From the time death first entered human history, men and women have wavered between belief in the immortality of the human soul, and a boding of its irrevocable mortality. On the whole, belief in survival beyond the grave has prevailed -

(1) Poets and Philosophers

Thinkers have seen intimations of immortality in many things, including: the perpetual renewal of nature, the cycles of winter and spring, the starry heavens, and even (in the case of William Wordsworth) in the recollection of early childhood -

> Thou, whose exterior semblance doth believe
>
> Thy Soul's immensity...
>
> Thou, over whom thy Immortality
>
> Broods like the Day, a Master o'er a slave,
>
> A presence which is not to be put by;
>
> Thou little Child, yet glorious in the might
>
> Of heaven-born freedom on thy being's height ...

But most commonly, man has found proof of his immortality within his own soul. As Emerson said, "The blazing evidence of immortality is our dissatisfaction with any other solution." To an inward-looking eye the human spirit seems so immense, and its yearning for endless life so insatiable, that anything other than continuance of existence beyond the grave becomes intolerable.

Joseph Addison (1672-1719) was once excited by Plato's explanation of this instinct, and he celebrated it thus -

> It must be so - Plato, thou reason'st well,
>
> Else whence this pleasing hope, this fond desire,
>
> This longing after immortality?
>
> Or whence this secret dread and inward horror
>
> Of falling into nought? Why shrinks the soul
>
> Back on herself and startles at destruction?
>
> - 'Tis the Divinity that stirs within us,
>
> 'Tis Heaven itself that points out an hereafter,
>
> And intimates Eternity to man.

The problem with all such "proofs" as those is that they may be no more than wishful thinking. Philosophers and poets, scientists and analysts, being themselves mortal, have all died, and not one has returned to show whether or not man truly is immortal.

This orbiting cemetery upon which we live, walking daily over the remains of countless millions who have died before us, appears to declare emphatically that the dead are as much imprisoned within it boundaries as are the living -

"Nature is called a mother, but she is a grave" (Alfred Vigny, c. 1830).

So if there is no voice to speak save that of the grave, or of the human soul, then it would seem that our hope of survival after death is illusory.

Against this unhappy prospect comes the exhilarating good news:

> "Our Saviour Christ Jesus has abolished death and brought life and immortality to light through the gospel" *(2 Ti 1:10)*.

The voice of the gospel speaks with assurance that death is not the end. Beyond the grave there is life!

But what kind of life?

(2) Spiritual or Physical?

Already in the time of the apostles that question was being raised, and there were people who argued for an exclusively "spiritual" resurrection. They rejected any suggestion that the body itself would actually come out of the grave. They reckoned those Christians who had died had already experienced resurrection, and they were already in full enjoyment of the bliss of Paradise, without need of any future raising of the body. Paul declared that such ideas were repugnant to the gospel (2 Ti 2:18); and Benjamin Atkinson comments -

> *"The resurrection of the dead is one of the great doctrines of Christ. Now see the subtlety of the serpent and the serpent's seed. They did not deny the resurrection (for that had been boldly and avowedly to confront the word of Christ), but they put a corrupt interpretation upon that doctrine, saying that the resurrection was past already, that what Christ spoke concerning the resurrection was to be understood mystically and by way of allegory, that it must be meant of a spiritual resurrection only. It is true, there is a spiritual resurrection, but to infer thence that there will not be a true and real resurrection of the body at the last day is to dash one truth of Christ in pieces against another ...*

> *Whoever takes away the doctrine of a future state overthrows the faith of Christians."*[41]

(3) Dualistic Heresy

This claim of a spiritual resurrection, with its corollary denial of a bodily resurrection, was probably based on a **dualistic concept**, in which matter and spirit were seen as mutually antagonistic. It was argued that since matter is evil and opposed to the spirit, then the human body must also be evil, and deserves to perish in the grave, so that the spirit might be at last released to serve God.

But scripture shows that personal life and full identity depend on the union of body and soul. Without one or the other we are incomplete (cp. 2 Co 5:1-5).

Hence there is no redemption of the body without the soul, nor any redemption of the soul without the body. This redemption of body and soul together has already begun (Ro 8:9-11) and will be completed when Christ returns (1 Th 5:23).

So scripture is emphatic: since the resurrection of Christ was bodily, so will be our resurrection -

> *"If we have been united with him in a death like his, we shall certainly be united with him in a resurrection like his" (Ro 6:4) ...*
>
> *"The body is for the Lord and the Lord for the body. And God raised the Lord and will also raise us by his power" (1 Co 6:13-14).*

(II) AFTER DEATH - WHAT?

Every human being lives with a particular goal in view. It is difficult to imagine any rational soul confronting life with no opinion at all about where it will all end. But people certainly have

---

[41] **Matthew Henry's Commentary**, in loc; 1953 reprint in 6 vols. by Marshall, Morgan, and Scott, London..

different ideas about what lies beyond death! Here are some of the most common -

(A) ATHEISTS

Atheists have as their goal the cemetery; their destiny, death. They hope only for dissolution of the flesh and extinction of consciousness. Their motto: "Our lives are but our funeral procession to the grave." They think that truly rational people must reject the idea of survival beyond the grave -

(1) A Rationalist's View

"I believe that when I die I shall rot, and nothing of my ego will survive. I am not young, and I love life. But I should scorn to shiver with terror at the thought of annihilation. Happiness is none the less true happiness because it must come to an end, nor do thought and love lose their value because they are not everlasting ... Man is a part (of this physical world). His body, like other matter, is composed of electrons and protons, which, so far as we know, obey the same laws as those not forming part of animals or plants ... What we call our 'thoughts' seem to depend upon the organisation of tracks in the brain in the same sort of way in which journeys depend upon roads and railways. The energy used in thinking seems to have a chemical origin ... Mental phenomena seem to be bound up with material structure. If this be so ... we cannot suppose that an individual's thinking survives bodily death, since that destroys the organisation of the brain, and dissipates the energy which utilised the brain tracks.

" ... Persons are part of the everyday world with which science is concerned, and the conditions which determine their existence are discoverable. A drop of water is not immortal; it can be resolved

> *into oxygen and hydrogen. If, therefore, a drop of water were to maintain that it had a quality of aqueousness which would survive its dissolution we should be inclined to be sceptical. In like manner we know that the brain is not immortal, and that the organised energy of a living body becomes, as it were, demobilised at death, and therefore not available for collective action. All the evidence goes to show that what we regard as our mental life is bound up with brain structure and organised bodily energy. Therefore it is rational to suppose that mental life ceases when bodily life ceases. The argument is only one of probability, but it is as strong as those upon which most scientific conclusions are based.*
>
> *" ... We all know that memory may be obliterated by an injury to the brain, that a virtuous person may be rendered vicious by encephalitis lethargical, and that a clever child can be turned into an idiot by lack of iodine. In view of such familiar facts, it seems scarcely probable that the mind survives the total destruction of the brain structure which occurs at death. It is not rational arguments, but emotions, that cause belief in a future life".* [42]

There is an element of truth in that last sentence. It is not possible to prove beyond all rational doubt that there is, or is not, an after-life. Professor Russell, basing his opinion on scientific data, thinks that probability favours the absolute finality of death. Christians raise two main objections: **firstly**, the proof of immortality offered by the resurrection of Christ; **secondly**, the instinct of immortality that is endemic in the human race.

---

[42] Bertrand Russell, Why I Am Not A Christian; Unwin Books, London, 1975; pg 47, 44-45, 71.

(2) A More Congenial View

As Pascal said, it takes a certain "strength of mind" to maintain an atheist's gloomy view of life[43]. Despite Professor Russell's claim, most people do feel that "thought and love" would lose most of their value if they are absolutely and irrevocably terminated by death. There seems little point in either thinking **or** loving if we have no more real substance or value than the drop of water the professor refers to. Few people are willing to equate themselves qualitatively with a dripping tap! Most would argue that water has no capacity to attribute to itself a quality of immortal aqueousness, whereas man does have such a capacity.

Nor are many people willing to allow that their mental processes are nothing more than a pre-determined set of chemical reactions in the brain cells, which is just another way of saying that brain and thought are inseparable, or that it is the brain alone that thinks. Most people feel that "I" think, and the brain is simply the tool "I" think with. The real "I" uses the brain as it uses all of the other organs of the body, but this self, or ego, or soul, or the true person, is distinct from any or all of those bodily parts.

True, the "I" needs the various components of the body, including the brain, through which to express itself, and if any of those parts are diseased or damaged the "I" may no longer be able to act or to communicate. But to hold a prisoner out of sight and incommunicado is no proof that he no longer exists!

This belief that "I" exist as an inhabitant of my body cannot be proved or disproved; but it is certainly more congenial to the average man or woman, and accords more with natural and universal instinct, than does any contrary opinion.

Few people have been able to endure the thought that nothing better awaits them, whether they are virtuous or wicked, than to be

---

[43] "Atheism shows strength of mind, but only to a certain extent." Pensees, # 333.

a foul feast for worms. Even when they have lacked any solid basis for their hope of immortality, most people have still preferred to protest with Longfellow -

> Tell me not, in mournful numbers,
>
> Life is but an empty dream!
>
> For the soul is dead that slumbers,
>
> And things are not what they seem.
>
> Life is real! Life is earnest!
>
> And the grave is not its goal;
>
> Dust thou art, to dust returnest,
>
> Was not spoken of the soul.
>
>   - A Psalm of Life (1835)

And ages before Longfellow, early peoples struggled to express their innate belief that death **could not** be the end, especially of a beautiful life. Thus, Hippostrate, a young Greek maiden in the 5th century BC, left this tender epitaph of her nurse, Melitta -

(To) Melitta, daughter of Apollodorus.

> Here lies beneath the earth Hippostrate's good nurse.
>
> And how Hippostrate now longs for you!
>
> I loved you so, dear nurse,
>
> And now, for all my life
>
> I'll honour you, though you lie below.
>
> If the good receive a prize in the underworld,

> You now, I know, enjoy first place with Pluto and Persephone[44].

Then approaching death has ever been a bitter awakener of reflections on what might lie beyond the grave. Thus in Plato's **Republic** (1.330D - 331B), the aged Cephalus gloomily ponders his possible fate -

> *"When the thought of his own death approaches a man, he feels fear and concern about things which he did not before. The stories that are told about the things in Hades, that the man who acted unjustly in this world must pay the penalty there, are laughed at until this time, but then the fear that they may be true racks his soul. And either because of the weakness of old age or because he is now closer to Hades, he himself sees those things more clearly and is filled with suspicion and terror[45] ..."*

In contrast with those uncertain longings and fears, Christians are far from feeling that they lack solid evidence for their hope of immortality. For all who joyfully believe in him, Christ has forever dispelled the mists, so that

> "The path of the righteous is like the light of dawn,
> which shines brighter and brighter until full day"
> *(Pr 4:18).*

(B) THE ANCIENTS

The ancients visualised future life in the form of disembodied spirits (or "shades"), confined within the endless twilight of Tartarus. In this shadowy nether world good and bad dwelt together, with little distinction between them, and little prospect of ever escaping their

---

[44] Quoted in Athenian Popular Religion, by Jon D. Mikalson; University of North Carolina Press; 1983; pg 79.

[45] Ibid., pg 80.

cheerless state. The dead had to reconcile themselves to a level of existence much inferior to the one they had enjoyed on earth.[46]

Homer tells the myth of a visit Odysseus made to the edge of Hade's realm. While there he was visited by the shade of the great Achilles, who said to his former prince -

> *"My Lord Odysseus, spare me your praise of Death. Put me on earth again, and I would rather be a serf in the house of some landless man, with little enough for himself to live on, than king of all these dead men that have done with life."*

That was in response to Odysseus' greeting:

> *"In the old days when you were on earth, we Argives honoured you as though you were a god;*

---

[46] My discussion here deals only with ancient beliefs about the after-life. There were many people who remained deeply unsure whether or not there was any existence beyond the grave. Thus Hyperides, an Athenian orator and prosecutor, delivered a funeral oration in 322 BC, commemorating those heroes who had perished in the Lamian War. In it he expressed his uncertainty about their fate, although plainly he leaned to the idea that they were being well rewarded -

"If death is like non-existence, then these men are freed from diseases and suffering and from other things which beset the life of a human being. But if men have perception in the house of Hades, and if they are cared for by the (gods), as we suspect they are, then it is reasonable to assume that those who defended the abused honours of the gods find the greatest care from (those same gods)." (6.43). (Ibid., pg 78,79.)

In the ancient world, of course, there were also atheists, as shown by a few references in the Bible, and especially in the OT Apocrypha. One of the best of the Apocryphal passages is Wisdom 2:1-25, which depicts the various claims of the atheists, and scornfully rejects them. (It should be noted though, that this ancient atheism, unlike that of modern atheists, was practical rather than theoretical. True theoretical atheism was almost unknown in the ancient world. The warnings in the following references all refer to practical atheists - Je 5:11-13; Am 9:10; Zp 9:12; Ps 14:1 ff; 53:1 ff).

> *and now, down here, you are a mighty prince among the dead. For you, Achilles, Death should have lost his sting."*

But how could death lose its sting for those who believed Homer's vision? This is how he describes the "shades" when they came to meet Odysseus -

> *Souls of the dead who had gone below came swarming up from Erebus - fresh brides, unmarried youths, old men with life's long suffering behind them, tender young girls still nursing this first anguish in their hearts, and a great throng of warriors killed in battle, their spear-wounds gaping yet and all their armour stained with blood. From this multitude of souls, as they fluttered to and fro ... there came a moaning that was horrible to hear."*[47]

Robert Graves describes the Homeric picture of the underworld thus:

> *"When ghosts descend to Tartarus, the main entrance to which lies in a grove of black poplars beside the Ocean stream, each is supplied by pious relatives with a coin laid under the tongue of its corpse. They are thus able to pay Charon, the miser who ferries them in a crazy boat across the Styx ... Penniless ghosts must wait for ever on the near bank, unless they have evaded Hermes, their conductor, and crept down by a back entrance ... A three-headed dog named Cerebus guards the opposite shore of the Styx, ready to devour living intruders or ghostly fugitives ... The first region of Tartarus contains the cheerless Asphodel Fields,*

---

[47] **The Odyssey**, Book 11, "The Book of the Dead"; tr by E.V. Rieu; Penguin Classics, 1958.

where souls of heroes stay without purpose among the throngs of less distinguished dead that twitter like bats ... Their one delight is in libations of blood poured to them by the living: when they drink they feel themselves almost men again ...[48]"

For the people of antiquity the dismal caverns ruled by Hades offered no joy. Can you imagine what it meant to live under the shadow of such a doleful future? Yet, rather than face the even worse horror of utter extinction, people still preferred to believe such bizarre myths. The consolation offered by the myths was meagre; but they did proffer some hope that a tenuous thread of life might survive the grave.

(C) HINDUS

Hindus seek "nirvana", the perfect happiness reached when a soul loses its personal identity and becomes absorbed into the supreme impersonal Soul of the universe. This loss of separate existence is thought to be the only way to find peace. It can be achieved only by a long process of trans-migration of the soul (re-incarnation). As the soul passes from generation to generation, being born each time into a station in life determined by the way the person lived in his previous incarnation, it is purified from wickedness, and may eventually escape this world altogether and so find "nirvana". Thus an ancient Hindu document (c. 2nd century BC), The Laws of Manu, talks about three kinds of sin: of the body, of the tongue, of the mind. Each sin leads to its own retributive incarnation in the person's next life; that is, his next life will reflect the dominant fault of his present existence. Hence, a person guilty of many verbal sins may, for example, be re-born as a twittering bird -

---

[48] The Greek Myths, Vols 1 & 2; Penguin Books, UK 1975; Vol 1, pg 120-121. The same work contains descriptions of other views of the after-life propounded by the ancient mythographers - all of them fantastic, and usually gloomy.

> *"A man obtains the result of a good or evil mental act in his mind, that of a verbal act in his speech, that of a bodily act in his body. In consequence of many sinful acts committed with his **body**, a man becomes in the next birth something inanimate; in consequence of sins committed by **speech**, a bird, or a beast; and in consequence of **mental** sins he is reborn in a low caste.[49]"*

Unless an escape can be found from this imprisoning cycle, each person is "enslaved by his actions, which follow him indefinitely ... (He) is condemned to be reborn (over and over); and as most human actions are tainted by malice, the risk of being reborn in a lower condition, ultimately as an animal, is greater than the possibility of achieving an exalted state ... Existence (life) flows as a torrent; man suffers passively the necessity of death in order that he be born and die, again and again. This is the basis of Indian pessimism, this frightful retributive accountability".[50]

(1) Only Two Certainties

Within the Hindu system then, there are only two certainties: **"Certain is death for the born, and certain is birth for the dead"** (Bhagavad Gita, 2:27). It was also thought, "Whatever state of existence is occupying your mind at the moment you leave your body in death, to that you will go, and in that condition you will be made".[51] Thus Geoffrey Parrinder writes:

> *"(The Universal Soul is known as 'Brahman'). Brahman is a neuter divine power, a holy power or energy, and it (is) used in the sense of the World-soul and universal divine being ... the one divine*

---

[49] Hinduism, by Louis Renou; pub. by George Raziller, New York, 1962; pg 117.
[50] Ibid., pg 43,44; emphasis mine.
[51] I have lost the source of this sentence.

essence ... Brahman is the soul-stuff that underlies all the visible world, from which all proceeds and to which all returns ...

The (Hindu sacred writings) teach the transmigration of the soul from one life on earth to another through rebirth. Whether the soul is finally to be identified with the divine or not, it is at present caught up in the web of deceit or illusion ... How is it, they ask, that heaven is not full up, with all the people that are dying? The answer is that souls return to earth again. Having worked out the reward or punishment of their earthly deeds, in the sky and the world of the ancestors, they then come back in the rain, become plants, and so re-enter human bodies in food ...

(Another view is that) a good or bad rebirth depends on one's previous actions. 'Those whose conduct has been good, will quickly attain some good birth, the birth of a Brahmin, or a ruler, or a merchant. But those whose conduct has been evil, will quickly attain an evil birth, the birth of a dog, or a hog, or an outcaste.' ... The proof of this (rebirth) is taken to be the indestructible nature of the soul, which is eternal and cannot die ...

... Indian thought tends to regard (this pattern of rebirth) as a chain by which the soul is bound in the wandering of transmigration, or a torturing wheel of birth and rebirth, or death and redeath. Great efforts are made to find release or salvation from this endless round of wandering. To achieve this, evil passions and illusions, 'the knots of the heart', must be broken and such a calm and passionless state attained that there is no remainder of 'karma'

(the thoughts, words, and acts of daily life) to bring one back to a bodily life".[52]

(2) Striving For Escape

A prayer to the Hindu deity Krishna expresses the idea that salvation is found by escape from the world:

> *"O Lord, destroy the miseries of this world! I am strung on a necklace of births and deaths ... How shall I reach the goal? My mind is overwhelmed by the powerful senses. I cannot shake off attachment to worldly pleasures ... Please control my senses and pull me out of this world of dangers ... I must throw off these shackles and catch hold of your mercy.[53]"*

Swami Prabhupada writes:

> *"We living entities are innumerable; there is no limit to our number. God, however, is one. He is also living as we are, but we are minute particles of that living force ... This godly particle, the soul or living force, is transmigrating from aquatics to trees and plants, and then from trees and plants to insect life, then to reptile life, then to the bodies of birds and beasts ... then human life ... Here is a junction: from this point we can again slide down into the cyclic process of evolution, or we can elevate ourselves to a godly life. The choice is up to us ...*
>
> *"We are part and parcel of God, but somehow or other we have fallen into this material existence: now we have to evolve in such a way that we can go back home, back to Godhead. That is the highest*

---

[52] The World's Living Religions, Pan Books, London, UK. 1964; pg 41-44.
[53] Back to Godhead magazine, # 51 (1973), pg 18. The full prayer consists of 24 verses. It is quite beautiful in parts.

> *perfection ... As soon as we get out of this illusion of identifying the soul with the body, (that is, when one can say,) 'I am not this body; I am spirit-soul, part and parcel of the Supreme Brahman,' he attains what is called Brahman-realisation. As soon as Brahman-realisation is attained, one becomes happy".*[54]

(3) An Awful Futility

The awful futility of these interminable cycles of birth and death, which at best can be escaped only by the sacrifice of personal awareness and self-identity, is all too plain. There is here no glad prospect, no beautiful heaven, no hope of personal enhancement. Nothing is left but a pessimistic notion that every created thing is irreparably evil, including one's own self. The soul can find rest only when by stern asceticism it is at last sundered from everything material and flows back into the primeval essence from which, aeons ago, it inadvertently broke away. Hinduism presents the ultimate irony: total salvation depends on total destruction; that is, on the annihilation of identity, the obliteration of self. The soul can find peace only by falling back into God, as a drop of spray falls back into the ocean, and is lost.

(D) MUSLIMS

Muslims anticipate a resurrection and judgment like that expected by Christians, as shown by this striking passage from the Koran -

> *Your Lord does not forget. He is the Lord of the heavens and the earth and all that is between them. Worship him, then, and be loyal in his service; for is there any other god like him?*
>
> *'What!' says man, 'When I am once dead, shall I be raised to life?'*

---

[54] Ibid. pg 25, 27.

> *Does man forget that We created him out of the void? ... (Therefore) We will deliver those who fear Us, but the wrongdoers shall be left to endure (the) torments (of hell) upon their knees ...*
>
> *There is none in the heavens or on earth but shall return to God in utter submission. He has kept strict count of all his creatures, and one by one they shall approach him on the Day of Resurrection. He will cherish those who accepted the true faith and were charitable in their life-time.*[55]*"*

So beyond the resurrection, for the devout Muslim, there exists a horribly literal hell, and a remarkably sensual paradise. Here are some further selections from the Koran -

(1) The Day of Judgment

Muslims anticipate, as Christians do, a coming Day of Judgment, in which the righteous and the unrighteous will be separated, the first to Paradise, the second to Punishment -

> *"Every soul shall taste death. You shall receive your rewards only on the Day of Resurrection. Whoever is spared the fire of Hell and is admitted to Paradise shall surely gain his end; for the life of this world is nothing but a fleeting vanity ... Because they disbelieved Our revelations and said: 'When we are turned to bones and dust, shall we be raised to life?' ... We shall gather them all on the Day of Resurrection, prostrate upon their faces, deaf, dumb, and blind. Hell shall be their home:*

---

[55] The Koran, Sura 19:66,67,72,93-96; translated by N.J.Dawood, Penguin Classics, 1980. These passages, and those that follow (all from the same translation), are only a few of the many references to the Last Day, the Resurrection, Judgment, Paradise, and Hell, contained in the Koran.

> *whenever its flames die down We will rekindle them into a greater fire" ... (Sura 3:185; 17:97-98)*
>
> *"The fate of each man We have bound about his neck. On the Day of resurrection We shall confront him with a book spread wide open, saying: 'Here is your book; read it. Enough for you this day that your own soul should call you to account.' " (Sura 17:13,14)*
>
> *"They also say: 'When will this promise be fulfilled, if what you say is true?' They must be waiting for the Trumpet's blast, which will overtake them while they are disputing ... And when the Trumpet sounds, they shall rise up from their graves and rush forth to their Lord. 'Woe to us!' they will say. 'Who has roused us from our resting- place?' ... On that day no soul shall suffer the least injustice. You shall be rewarded only according to your deeds. On that day the dwellers of Paradise shall think of nothing but their bliss. Together with their wives, they shall recline in shady graves upon soft couches. They shall have fruits and all that they desire." (Sura 36:48- 49, 51-52, 54-57).*

And on the Day of Judgment, the Koran teaches:

> *"When that which is coming comes - and no soul shall then deny its coming - some shall be abased and others exalted. When the earth shakes and quivers and the mountains crumble away and scatter abroad into fine dust, you shall be divided into three multitudes: those on the right (blessed shall be those on the right); those on the left (damned shall be those on the left); and those to the fore (foremost shall be those!) ...*
>
> *They shall recline on jewelled couches face to face, and there shall wait on them immortal youths with*

> *bowls and ewers and a cup of purest wine (that will neither pain their heads nor take away their reason); with fruits of their own choice and flesh of fowls that they relish. And theirs shall be the dark-eyed houris, chaste as hidden pearls ... We created the houris and made them virgins, loving companions for those on the right hand ...*
>
> *As for those on the left hand (wretched shall be those on the left hand!), they shall dwell amidst scorching winds and seething water: in the shade of pitch black smoke ... (For they said), 'When we are once dead and turned to dust and bones, shall we, with all our forefathers, be raised to life?' Say (to them): 'This present generation, as well as the generation that passed before it, shall be brought together on an appointed day. As for you sinners who deny the truth, you shall eat the fruit of the Zaqqum tree and fill your bellies with it. You shall drink boiling water: yet you shall drink it as the thirsty camel drinks.' Such shall be their fare on the Day of Reckoning." (Sura 56:1-10,15-23,35-38,41-43,47-56).*

Further, on the same theme the Koran says:

> *"The righteous shall return to a blessed retreat. They shall enter the gardens of Eden, whose gates shall open to receive them. Reclining there with bashful virgins for companions, they shall feast on abundant fruit and drinks ... But doleful shall be the return of the transgressors. They shall burn in the fire of Hell, a dismal resting-place. There let them taste their drink: scalding water, festering blood, and other putrid things ...*
>
> *"Fixed is the Day of Judgment. On that day the Trumpet shall be sounded and you shall come in*

multitudes. The gates of heaven shall swing open and the mountains shall pass away and become like vapour. Hell will lie in ambush, a home for the transgressors. There they shall abide long ages; there they shall taste neither refreshment nor any drink, save boiling water and decaying filth: a fitting recompense ... We shall say: 'Taste this: you shall have nothing but mounting torment!'

"As for the righteous, they shall surely triumph. Theirs shall be gardens and vineyards, and high-bosomed maidens for companions: a truly overflowing cup." (Suras 38:49- 52,55-57; 78:17-26,30-34).

The joys of Paradise are often described in the Koran, but always in rather earthy terms:

"The true servants of Allah shall be well provided for, feasting on fruits, and honoured in the gardens of delight. Reclining face to face upon soft couches, they shall be served with a goblet filled at a gushing fountain, white, and delicious to those who drink it. It will neither dull their senses nor befuddle them. They shall sit with bashful, dark-eyes virgins, as chaste as the sheltered eggs of ostriches ...

"As for the righteous, they shall dwell in peace together amidst gardens and fountains, arrayed in rich silks and fine brocade. Yes, and We shall wed them to dark-eyed houris. Secure against all ills, they shall call for every kind of fruit; and, having died once, they shall die no more ... In fair gardens the righteous shall dwell in bliss, rejoicing in what their Lord will give them ... They shall recline on couches ranged in rows. To dark-eyes houris We shall wed them ... Fruits we shall give them, and such meats as they desire. They will pass from hand

> *to hand a cup inspiring no idle talk, no sinful urge;*
> *and there shall wait on them young boys of their*
> *own as fair as virgin pearls."   (Suras 37:40-49;*
> *44:51-56; 52:17-20,22-24)*

That seems to be a sexist heaven, with a heavy bias toward male bliss[56]. Muslims apparently take it seriously, although the more thoughtful among them must surely try to interpret Muhammad's words symbolically rather than literally.[57] Yet the picture remains of a Paradise that has nothing higher to offer than any wealthy Muslim male can already enjoy. It is in the end a bleak vision.

So we are left now with one other major view to consider, of what lies beyond the grave, and that is the Christian. That will be the theme of the next chapter.

---

[56] The Koran does offer a paradisiacal reward for righteous women, but its details are not spelled out, as they are for men (whose reward is often described as being wedded to beautiful virgin wives, the dark-eyed houris of the Muslim heaven; but where that leaves their former earthly wives, is not stated.) Rewards for righteous women are spoken of, though vaguely, in Sura 4:124; 33:29,35; and perhaps elsewhere as well. But unless the words of the Koran are spiritualised, so that all gender is removed from them, the Islamic paradise remains prejudiced toward male pleasures.

[57] Thus A. Yusef Ali, in The Holy Qur'an - a Translation and Commentary, declares: "To write about the Muslim heaven adequately ... is all the more necessary, as some ignorant critics of Islam imagine that Islam postulates a sensual heaven, and they press into service some garbled versions of what some of our own more material-minded brethren have said on the subject" (pg 1464; pub. by American Trust Publications, 1977.) Yusef Ali, in his notes, presents a high view of Islam, and he obviously possesses a great nobility of spirit, which itself has been strongly influenced by western (and hence Christian) culture. But it is difficult to escape the impression that he is not so much explaining what the Koran says on these matters, as evading what it says. And it is clear from his own comments that there are many Muslims who do indeed take the Koranic statements about Paradise literally.

CHAPTER EIGHT

OUR GLORIOUS GOAL

Sir Isaac Newton, the great 17th century physicist and mathematician, was also a devout Christian, filled with wonder at the glories of God's creation. He maintained his curiosity, his scientific inquiry, to the very end of his life. It is reported that his last words were -

> *"I do not know what I may appear to the world. But to myself, I seem to have been only a boy playing on the seashore, diverting myself in now and then finding a smoother pebble or a prettier shell than ordinary, whilst the great ocean of truth lay all undiscovered before me."*

We may well feel the same, as we continue our study of the mystery of the resurrection and the glorious hope God has given us in Christ. There is always a haunting sense that we are only splashing in the shallows, or that we have seen nothing more than shadows of a magnificent splendour.

But even the shadows of this glory are exhilarating. So let us press on. Here we are going to contrast the various heathen goals we looked at in your previous lesson with the goal God has given us in Christ. We shall answer two questions: what is that goal; and what guarantee do we have that this goal is true, while the others are false?

(I) THE GOAL

Our goal is the return of Christ:

> *"Our commonwealth is in heaven, and from it we await a Saviour, the Lord Jesus Christ ... So Christ, having been offered once to bear the sins of many, will appear a second time, not to deal with sin, but to save those who are eagerly waiting for him ... We await our blessed hope, the appearing of the glory of our great God and Saviour Jesus Christ" (Ph 3:20; He 9:28; Tit 2:13).*

In that majestic promise we find three things -

(A) RESURRECTION

See 2 Co 5:1-4.

Unlike the atheist, we do not look for extinction; unlike the Hindu, we do not look for fusion with some cosmic force; unlike the Moslem, we do not look for sensual indulgence; rather, we look for the **resurrection**, in which we shall receive a new body, a heavenly body, so that we shall be more alive, more aware, more **real** than we are now, and more gloriously able to serve our Lord.

This is no doubt a great mystery, this promise of personal survival beyond the grave; and for that reason many people refuse to consider it. If they do not actually reject the idea, they say that since it is impossible to prove or disprove, why waste time discussing the matter. Two great writers offer a pungent reply –

(1) A Foolish Evasion

(a) Athenagoras

Athenagoras was an Athenian philosopher and Christian, who flourished during the latter part of the second century (that is, less than 100 years after the death of the apostle John). With artistry and grace he wrote numerous works arguing for the truth of the gospel, at least one of which was presented in the year 177 to the Emperor Aurelius. All but two of his writings have perished, and one of those deals with **The Resurrection of the Dead**. Plato, in his **Phaedo**, offers conjectures about possible survival beyond the grave; but Athenagoras is the first known Greek philosopher to express certainty that death is not the end.

Athenagoras drew on aspects of nature, life, and God, to establish the truth of the Christian doctrine of the resurrection of the dead. Here are some lines from his chapter dealing with the evidence of human nature. They have been described as possessing "calm sublimity (excelling) all that ever came before from an Athenian (on life after death)." It was inconceivable to Athenagoras that any sensible person could ignore this doctrine, or any longer doubt it -

> *"Confident of these things, no less than of those which have already come to pass, and reflecting on our own nature, we are content with a life associated with neediness and corruption, as suited to our present state of existence, and we steadfastly hope for a continuance of being in immortality; and this we do not take without foundation from the inventions of men, feeding ourselves on false hopes, but our belief rests on a most infallible guarantee - the purpose of him who fashioned us, according to which he made man of an immortal soul and a body ... (For) we know well that God would not have fashioned such a being, and furnished him with everything belonging to perpetuity, had he not intended that what was so created should continue in perpetuity ...*
>
> *And we shall make no mistake in saying, that the final cause of an intelligent life and rational judgment, is to be occupied uninterruptedly with those objects to which the natural reason is chiefly and primarily adapted, and to delight unceasingly in the contemplation of **him who is**, and of his decrees, notwithstanding that the majority of men, because they are affected too passionately and too*

> *violently by things below, pass through life without attaining this object".*[58]

We may well ask, in a world full of doubt and despair, where did the philosopher find such unwavering confidence that he would conquer the grave? What new thing had come among men, to engender such assurance? It was of course, the gospel of Christ, which suddenly gave new meaning and power to all of the pieces of evidence that had given previous generations some vague hope that life might somehow continue after death.

(b) Blaise Pascal

The great French mathematician and philosopher, mentioned in the Preface to this series, was singularly scathing of those who thought it was pointless to discuss the resurrection -

> *"I will tell them something I have often said, that their negligence is insufferable. We are not concerned here with the trifling interests of some stranger, that we should adopt this attitude; the matter concerns ourselves and our all.*

> *"The immortality of the soul is of such consequence to us, and affects us so deeply, that we would have to be totally devoid of feeling before we could be indifferent as to whether it is true. Our every thought and action must follow such different paths according as there are or are not eternal joys for which to hope, that it is impossible to take one step with good sense and sound judgment unless our course is regulated by our view of this point, which should be our final end.*

---

[58] Ante-Nicene Fathers, Vol 2, Fathers of the Second Century; pg 155,156, 162; Eerdmans Pub. Co., Michigan; 1979 reprint.

> "Thus our first interest and first duty is to enlighten ourselves upon this subject, whereon all our conduct depends ... I take a (poor) view of those who (neglect) to do all they can to discover whether this belief is one of those which people receive with credulous simplicity, or one of those which, although obscure in themselves, have a firm and unshakeable foundation.

> "This neglect in a matter which concerns themselves, their eternity, their all, moves me to anger rather than to pity; it astonishes and frightens me; I regard it as a monstrosity ... The doubter, therefore, who does not make this search is at once most unfortunate and altogether in the wrong. If, in addition, he is placid and content, admits to being so, and even boasts of the fact, then I can find no words to describe so ridiculous a person."[59]

The above comments lie near the beginning of the **Pensees**. They are followed by many other penetrating remarks (scattered here and there among the nearly one thousand fragments) that offer cogent reasons for belief in the immortality of the soul and the need to prepare for life after death. Yet for all that, Pascal says -

> "I shall not undertake here to prove by natural reasons either the existence of God, or the Trinity, or the immortality of the soul, or anything of that sort; not only because I should feel insufficiently able to find in nature arguments with which to convince hardened atheists, but also because such knowledge without Jesus Christ is useless and sterile ... All who seek God apart from Jesus Christ, and who confine themselves to nature, either discover no satisfactory light or end by devising a

---

[59] Op. cit. Fragment # 11.

means of knowing and serving God without a mediator. Thereby they fall either into atheism or into deism[60], two things of which the Christian religion has an almost equal horror" (**Fragment # 17**).

Those words are simple truth. No certain evidence of immortality, nor of the resurrection, can be gained from either nature or mere thought. In the end, proof of personal survival will be found only by those who are willing to commit themselves to Christ.

If immortality has not been brought to light by him, then neither has it been revealed by anyone else[61].

But for the Christian, faith in Christ brings its own authentication. We **believe**; therefore we **know**. Christ has revealed himself to us through faith, making known to us his own triumph over death, and planting within us the certainty that we shall be given the same victory.

---

[60] "Deism" as used here means an abstract proof of God's existence, based on philosophical thought, apart from the biblical revelation; hence it is devoid of the supernatural element, and of the element of redemption, which are integral to Christianity.

[61] Even the Koran recognises Jesus as a special Messenger sent by God to bring the "Gospel" to mankind, and by many "signs" (including raising the dead) to establish the truth of that "Gospel". The Koran also teaches that Jesus was "raised up" by God, and taken back into heaven. See Sura 3 -

"God said, 'Jesus, I will take thee to Me, and I will raise thee to Me ... I will set thy followers above the unbelievers till the Resurrection Day' ... " And Sura 4 - "God raised him (Jesus) up to Him ... There is not one of the People of the Book but will assuredly believe in him before his death, and on the Resurrection Day he will be a witness against them ... " And Sura 57 - "We sent Jesus son of Mary, and gave unto him the Gospel ... O Believers, fear God, and believe in His Messenger ..." And Sura 3 - "(Jesus) will also heal the blind and the leper ... and bring life to the dead, by the leave of God ... "

There are numerous similar references to Jesus scattered through the Koran.

When we turn to scripture, however, it becomes plain that no one was fully sure how the resurrection would take place. In one passage Paul likens it to what happens in a garden (1 Co 15:35-46); but in another (2 Co 5:1-4), he replaces that metaphor with two others -

(2) Two Lovely Metaphors

(a) Like a new house (vs 1-4a)

Our present bodies, says Paul are like a rough desert tent; but in the resurrection they will be like a building, a palace, fashioned directly by God. This analogy tells two things about the resurrection body: its greatness, and its permanence.

Firstly, see how **great** a change will occur, as though a tent were transformed into a palace. Let no one imagine that the resurrection will be a small work! The metamorphosis of the saints will be sublime. The ransomed and reconstituted servants of God will each be pervaded by supernal glory.

Then notice the **permanence** of the resurrection body. It will not be temporary and easily "dismantled", like the "tent" that is my present body; but my new "house" will, says Paul, be "eternal in the heavens". It may change "from glory to glory", but it can never be destroyed!

Such knowledge removes the fear of death, which now becomes (for us) merely a necessary prelude to receiving our new "house". We are happy to accept the demolition of this mean "earthly tent" in which we presently live, so that we may inherit the "building" we shall have "from God".

Origen, the great third century Christian apologist, comments:

> *"Concerning the body also, the apostle writes: 'We have a house not made with hands, eternal in the heavens (that is, 'in the mansions of the blessed').' Now from that saying we may construct a likeness of that body. How pure, how refined, how glorious are its qualities in comparison with other familiar*

> *celestial bodies, which, although they are brilliant in their splendour, were nevertheless made with hands, and are visible to our sight. But of that body it is said that it is a house not made with hands, but eternal in the heavens.*
>
> *"Since, then, 'those things that are seen are temporal, but those things that are not seen are eternal,' all those bodies that exist either on earth or in heaven, which are capable of being seen, and have been made by hands, but are not eternal, will be far excelled in glory by that body, which is not visible, nor made with hands, but is eternal. From this comparison you may conceive how great is the beauty, and splendour, and brilliance of a spiritual body ...*
>
> *"However, we should never doubt that God, who made this present body, will be able to transform its nature into those qualities of refinement, and purity, and splendour, which will characterise the spiritual body".* [62]

(b) *Like a new garment (vs 3-4)*

If the first metaphor had been left to stand alone, an impression might have been made that there will be no common identity between the resurrection body and my present body - for what link can there be between a "tent" and a "mansion"? So Paul introduces the idea of a garment. But he gives it a surprising twist. The analogy is not that of changing one garment for another, nor even that of discarding an old garment in order to replace it with a new one. Rather, he talks about adding a new garment, which then absorbs and transforms the old:

---

[62] De Principiis, Bk 3, ch 6; paraphrased.

> *"not that we would be <u>unclothed</u>, but that we would be <u>further</u> clothed, so that what is mortal may be swallowed by life."*

That analogy stresses what is demanded elsewhere in scripture: unless the whole person, body, soul, and spirit is involved, the resurrection will fail. Man is a union of body and soul, and his continuance as a viable and fully personal being depends upon the maintenance of that union. It is disrupted by death, and remains broken during the intermediate state between death and the resurrection - a period during which Paul thinks of himself as being "naked" - but it will be restored at the moment of resurrection.

Thus one of the main purposes of the resurrection is made clear: to re-unite body and spirit, and to enable the risen saints to enter into their proper heritage.

Does that mean the intermediate state is inferior to our present state? No, only that it is inferior to our ultimate state.

Hence Paul said that he

> *"would rather be away from the body and at home with the Lord;" for while we are "at home in the body we are away from the Lord" (vs 6, 8).*

He also says elsewhere:

> *"to die is gain ... my desire is to depart and be with Christ, for that is far better" (Ph 1:21-23).*

Plainly then, death will bring us into a condition of joyous union with Christ, and into a state that is superior to life on earth. But just as plainly, that disembodied state must impose severe limitations on the capacity of the soul to express itself, to act creatively, and to maintain a unique personal existence. Those disabilities cannot be rectified except by a resurrection of the body.

However, remember that analogies of the resurrection (whether those of a "building" and a "garment", or any others that are used in scripture) should not be pressed too far. They are illustrations not doctrines. Scripture affirms that the resurrection will require an awesome display of divine power, that it will be stunning in its results, and that it will require in some way the raising-up of the same body that was "sown" in the ground - but in the end we are still left with two mysteries: how can such an incredible feat be done, even by God; and, what will we look like in our resurrected state? Neither of those questions is answered in the Bible. It is simply affirmed that the might of God will easily accomplish the task of bringing all of the dead out of their graves; and, although "it does not yet appear what we shall be, we know that when Christ appears we shall be like him, for we shall see him as he is" (1 Jn 3:2).

You should also note that none of this is given merely to gratify curiosity. As always, the prime purpose of scripture is ethical, not abstract; it is concerned with daily life, not with mere ideas. So John, having revealed that we shall see Jesus when he comes, and that the sight of him will change us into his likeness, was not content to stop there with a happy hallelujah! He at once gave his readers (and us) the admonition:

> *"Every one who thus hopes in Christ purifies himself as he is pure"* (vs 3).

(B) EXAMINATION (5:10)

For we must all appear before the judgment seat of Christ, that each one may receive what is due to him for the things done in the body, whether good or evil" (see also Ro 14:10)

There is a tendency, when Christians think about this passage (and others like it) to focus at once on the threat of punishment. That is certainly part of Paul's intention. But why make it the central part? A better way to view the passage is not as provoking fear of judgment, but rather as arousing in us a godly ambition to receive God's promised reward. The emphasis is hope, not dread.

Hence Paul's bold and exhilarating words:

> "We are always of good courage; we know that while we are at home in the body we are away from the Lord, for we walk by faith, not by sight. We are of good courage, and ... whether we are at home or away, we make it our aim to please him" (vs 6-9).

Dismiss the idea that God is quicker to condemn than he is to commend, or that he is more tardy with reward than he is with revenge. At worst, the positions are nicely balanced:

> "We must all appear before the judgment seat of Christ, so that each one may receive good or evil, according to what he has done in the body" (vs 10, RSV).

There is no partiality there! At best, "good" precedes "evil", so we may be sure that while the Lord cannot overlook things that merit his wrath, he will be even more ready to honour all the good we have done (cp. He 6:10). Righteousness presses more urgently upon the Father than unrighteousness!

So then, while the warning should cause us to be watchful against sin; but the promise should even more fill us with bold and expectant hope.

Which leads to the next idea -

(C) COMPENSATION (4:16-17)

In a letter to a lady, Chrysostom wrote:

> "Do not therefore be cast down. For there is only one thing, Olympias, which is really terrible, only one real trial, and that is sin; and I have never ceased continually harping upon this theme; but as for all other things, plots, enmities, frauds, calumnies, insults, accusations, confiscation, exile, the keen sword of the enemy, the peril of the deep, warfare of the whole world, or anything else you like to name, they are but idle tales. For whatever the nature of these things may be they are transitory

> *and perishable, and operate in a mortal body without doing any injury to the vigilant soul.*
>
> *"Therefore the blessed Paul, desiring to prove the insignificance both of the pleasures and sorrows relating to this life, declared the whole truth in one sentence when he said, 'For the things which are seen are temporal.' Why then dost thou fear temporal things, which pass away like a river[63]?"*

When Chrysostom wrote those words to his dear friend he was himself suffering bitterly in exile. But no sorrow could extinguish the joy that Paul's numinous vision had kindled in the aged bishop's heart. So he encouraged Olympias to be brave in her own trials, to open her eyes to see the invisible, and to look for the glittering prize described by Paul, that "eternal weight of glory beyond all comparison".

It is impossible to read Paul's description of what God has prepared for his church without feeling that the apostle is stretching language beyond its limits. He has seen a vision that defies captivity by words. And ever since, his readers have felt their own imaginations being stirred, and their spirits challenged, to penetrate the veil, to see into the future, and to be thrilled by the same vision of heavenly splendour.

Chrysostom typically returned to this theme many times:

> *"Wherefore Paul also called their afflictions 'light'; not from the nature of the events, but because of the*

---

[63] Chrysostom was Patriarch of Constantinople from A.D. 398-407. His real name was John; but he was called Chrysostom ("Golden-mouthed") in honour of his magnificent skill as a preacher. He wrote at least 17 letters to Olympias, a deaconess. The above selection is from the first, as found in The Nicene and Post-Nicene Fathers, First Series, Vol 9; edited by Philip Schaff; Wm. B. Eerdmans Pub. Co, Michigan; reprint 1978; pg 289. Other quotations from Chrysostom in this unit are drawn from, or based on, the same series.

> *mind of the combatants, and the hope of the future. 'For our light affliction,' saith he, 'worketh an eternal weight of glory, while we look not at the things which are seen, but at the things which are not seen.' For if to sailors the waves and the seas, to soldiers their slaughters and wounds, to husbandmen the winters and the frosts, to boxers the sharp blows, be light and tolerable things, all of them, for the hope of those rewards which are temporary and perishing; much more when heaven is set forth, and the unspeakable blessings, and the eternal rewards, will no one feel any of the present hardships. Or if any account it, even thus, to be toilsome, the suspicion comes of nothing but their own remissness.*[64]"

And Matthew Henry wrote:

> The prospect of eternal life and happiness kept them from fainting, and was a mighty support and comfort. As to this observe: the apostle and his fellow-sufferers saw their afflictions working towards heaven, and that they would end at last (vs 16-17), whereupon they weighted things aright in the balance of the sanctuary; they did as it were put the heavenly glory in one scale and their earthly sufferings in the other; and, pondering things in their thoughts, they found afflictions to be light, and the glory of heaven to be 'a far more exceeding weight'. That which sense was ready to pronounce heavy and long, grievous and tedious, faith

---

[64] Ibid., Vol. 10, Homily 23, on Matthew, pg 162. Augustine, and other church Fathers, wrote quite similar passages. I can recall reading them, but I have lost the references

perceived to be light and short, and but for a moment.⁶⁵ "

Johann Bengel (1687-1752) reckoned that there was in Paul's statement "a noble oxymoron" - which means a combination within one phrase of terms that are usually contradictory, such as "a cheerful pessimist", or "honour grounded in dishonour". Bengel himself gives an example: **"It is truly the height of <u>dignity</u> to be treated with <u>indignity</u> for Christ's sake."** In our text, Bengel sees the following contrasts-

just now   -   eternal

lightness   -   weight

affliction   -   glory

excessive   -   super-excessive

This last oxymoron (**excessive/super-excessive**) is translated in the RSV, **beyond all comparison**; but Bengel says that the ide' is rather: "even that **affliction** which is **excessive** when compared with other less afflictions (such as the 'unbearable' afflictions described by Paul in 1:8), is yet light compared with the exceeding glory.⁶⁶"

And Albert Barnes also comments on the passage:

> *"(It) abounds with intensive and emphatic expressions, and manifests that the mind of the writer was labouring to convey ideas which language, even after all the energy of expression which he could command, would very imperfectly communicate. The trials which Paul endured, to many persons would have seemed to be anything else but light. They consisted of want, and danger, and contempt, and stoning, and toil, and weariness,*

---

⁶⁵ Commentary, in loc.
⁶⁶ Op. cit., in loc.

and the scorn of the world, and constant exposure to death by land and by sea ... Yet these trials, though continued through many years, and constituting, as it were, his very life, he speaks of as the lightest conceivable thing when compared with that eternal glory which awaited him.

"He strives to get an expression as emphatic as possible to show that, in his estimation; (his afflictions) were not worthy to be named in comparison with the eternal weight of glory ... (So he writes) 'kath hyperboleen eis hyperboleen'. *There is not to be found anywhere a more energetic expression than this. The word* 'hyperboleen' *here used (whence our word hyperbole) means properly, a throwing, casting, or throwing beyond. In the NT it means excess, excellence, eminence ... The phrase* 'kath hyperboleen' *means exceedingly, super-eminently ...*

"This expression would have been by itself intensive in a high degree. But this was not sufficient to express Paul's sense of the glory which was laid up for Christians. It was not enough for him to use the ordinary highest expression for the superlative to denote the value of the object in his eye. He therefore coins an expression, and adds 'eis hyperboleen'. *It is not merely eminent, but it is eminent unto eminence; excess unto excess, a hyperbole unto hyperbole - one hyperbole heaped on another, and the expression means that it is 'exceeding exceedingly' glorious ...*

"(It) means that all hyperboles fail of expressing that eternal glory which remains for the just. It is infinite and boundless. You may pass from one degree to another; from one sublime height to another; but still an infinity remains beyond.

> *Nothing can describe the uppermost height of that glory; nothing can express its infinitude ... So the account stands in the view of Paul; and with this balance in favour of the eternal glory, he regarded afflictions as mere trifles, and made it the grand purpose of his life to gain the glory of the heavens. What wise man, looking at the account, would not do likewise[67]?"*

(II) THE GUARANTEE

If our **goal** is to obtain that **"immensely great and everlasting weight of glory"**, what **guarantee** do we have that we are not pursuing an illusion?

In the passage we are discussing, Paul suggests that we have a two-fold guarantee -

(A) THE WITNESS OF THE SPIRIT

> *"He who has prepared us for this very thing is God, who has given us the Spirit as a guarantee" (2 Co 5:5).*

The Greek word translated **guarantee** is **arrabon**. William Barclay calls it "a foretaste of what is to come", and he adds: "the word **arrabon** has one of the most human and interesting backgrounds of all NT words."

---

[67] Op. cit., in loc. Barnes' remarks on almost every word of this part of 2 Corinthians are so eloquent and moving, so rich with devotion and insight, I would be delighted to quote his commentary on these three verses in full - but it runs to eight columns of small print. So I may only hope you will be able to obtain and read the original. As Barnes himself says: "In this exceedingly interesting passage, which is worthy of the deepest study of Christians, Paul has set in most beautiful and emphatic contrast the trials of this life and the glories of heaven."

It is used three times in the NT - 1 Co 1:22; 5:5; Ep 1:14 - and in each case it expresses the witness and work of the Holy Spirit in the believer's life, both now and in the future.

Arrabon came into the Greek language from a legal and trading term used by the Phoenicians. It was used in three ways

- ➢ a **pledge**: that is, a refundable deposit, such as could be required by a person from whom you might wish to hie, say, a boat. The idea here is that the **arrabon** will be returned when the required action is completed.
- ➢ a first **instalment**; such as a person today might make on a hire purchase contract. The **arrabon** here is a financial deposit, and it represents a guarantee of full payment later.
- ➢ a **validation**; that is, a payment which had the effect of making a contract legally valid, and which obligated both parties to complete the contract and to protect it from the claims of any third party.

Barclay presents the following examples of its use, taken from ancient Greek papyri -

> *"A woman was selling a cow and she received one thousand drachmae as an arrabon that the remainder of the price would be paid. Certain dancing girls were being hired for a village festival and they are paid so many drachmae in advance as an arrabon, with the proviso that this already paid sum will be taken into account when the final payment is made after the performance is given. And - a rather amusing instance - a man writes, 'Regarding Lampon, the mouse-catcher, I paid him for you as arrabon eight drachmae in order that he may catch the mice while they are with young.' The advance payment is made, as a guarantee of full*

> *payment, so that Lampon will get on with the job of catching mice while the going is good[68]!"*

Other commentators link **arrabon** with ancient customs relating to the conveyancing of property, in which the seller would give the buyer a handful of earth or part of the thatch of the house as a token that the sale was binding, and that the whole property, of which the buyer thus received a part, would be handed over in due course.

Something of all those ideas is associated with Paul's use of **arrabon**. It carries the thought of a legal contract into which God has entered with the Christian, thus binding himself to fulfil all that he has promised, and especially to fulfil the promise of the resurrection. The gift of the Spirit activates and validates the divine promise for each person who receives that gift. By giving us his Spirit, God "put his seal upon us" (2 Co 1:22), and thus "guarantees our inheritance until we acquire possession of it, to the praise of his glory" (Ep 1:13-14).

The Holy Spirit as an **arrabon** also becomes for us a foretaste of that inheritance. His presence is like a handful of heaven's earth. The life the Holy Spirit imparts to us has the same quality as the life we shall receive in the resurrection. It is an advance deposit of that life, already at work in the believer's spirit and in his flesh.

Sensing this **arrabon** of life, we cannot doubt that the full measure will come to us in God's time. As Chrysostom said:

"If God did not purpose to give the whole, he would never have chosen to give the 'earnest' and to waste it without purpose or result."

But the divine **arrabon** is also a returnable pledge. When faith is realised by sight, and hope is fulfilled in the inheritance, and we stand face to face with Christ, we shall no longer need the

---

[68] New Testament Words; SCM Press Ltd. London, 1964; pg 58-59.

Consular as we need him now (cp. Jn 14:16-17, 26, 28-29; 16:17; etc).

There is also a further idea linked with **arrabon** - it presupposes an equally serious intention by both parties. The Christian who accepts the guarantee of the Spirit becomes as bound as God is to fulfil the terms of the contract. If the contract is violated, then the **arrabon** must be forfeited.

Hence, Chrysostom said on Ephesians 1:14 -

> *"Paul here makes the thing already bestowed a sure token of the promise of those which are yet to come. For this reason he further calls it an **earnest** (cp. also 2 Co 1:22), for an earnest is a part of the whole. Christ hath purchased what we are most concerned in, our salvation; and hath given us an earnest in the meanwhile. Why then did he not give us the whole at once? Because neither have we, on our part, done the whole of our work. We have believed. This is a beginning; and he too on his part hath given an earnest. When we show our faith by our works, then he will add the rest.*
>
> *"Nay, more, he hath given yet another pledge, his own blood, and hath promised another still. In the same way as in case of war between nation and nation they give hostages, just so hath God also given his Son as a pledge of peace and solemn treaties; and, further, the Holy Spirit also which is from him. For they that are indeed partakers of the Spirit, know that he is the earnest of our inheritance.*[69]*"*

---

[69] Op cit., Vol 13, pg 56. Note also, in modern Greek arrabon is used of an engagement ring; that is, a pledge of betrothal.

This arrabon of the Holy Spirit, this guarantee of future redemption, is possessed by all who have been born again by the Spirit; but it is especially the property of those who have received a charismatic baptism in the Spirit. This is made certain by comparing Ep 1:13-14 with Ac 19:1-7; nor can there be any doubt that the church at Corinth would today be known as a pentecostal church. It cannot be without significance that Paul spoke of the Holy Spirit being a guarantee, a divine arrabon, to people whom he knew had experienced a pentecostal baptism in the Spirit. To such Christians in particular, as they stand worshipping with the spirit (1 Co 14:15), rejoicing in the fullness of the Spirit, the promise of God is personally validated, and they know that the dynamic they feel is the dynamic of the coming resurrection!

(B) THE WITNESS OF FAITH

> *"So we are always of good courage, for we know that while we are at home in the body we are away from the Lord; for we walk by faith, not by sight"*
> *(2 Co 5:6-7).*

Some things only faith can adequately attest. But since I have already mentioned this above, and since the concept of the evidence faith brings has been discussed in some detail in the VCC lesson series on the **Authority of the Bible**, I will write no more on this subject here. Except to suggest that you read again the relevant parts of those lessons, and to say that, finally, proof of the resurrection and of the inheritance promised to the righteous, comes only to those who step by faith into the promise of God. To all who believe it, that promise wonderfully authenticates itself; but to those who doubt, the promise remains dead, and no vision is given.

CONCLUSION

If all of these things are true, then a two-fold response from us surely becomes inevitable -

    (1) To live with a vision of the invisible - see 2 Co 4:17-18.

(2) To live with one aim: to please God - see 2 Co 5:8-9.

As Christians we neither struggle to hold on to life at all costs, nor do we pine to die. To us, both are irrelevant. Our goal is simply to please God. If it is the pleasure of God that we should continue to live in this world, then such is our delight, whatever the world may hold for us. If it is the pleasure of God that we should die, and go to be with Christ, then this too is our delight, and we face death with joy. We sing with Paul:

> *"It is my eager expectation and hope that I shall not be at all ashamed, but that with full courage now as always Christ will be honoured in my body, whether by life or death. For to me to live is Christ, and to die is gain!" (Ph 1:20-24).*

One of the most colourful figures in English history is Sir Walter Raleigh. He was distrusted and feared by King James, who ordered his execution in 1618. Raleigh entered the Palace Yard with good humour. He joked with the executioner, until calmly giving the signal himself for the axe to fall. Perhaps this poem, found in his Bible after his death, explains his courage -

> Even such is Time, which takes in trust
>
> Our youth, our joys, our all we have,
>
> And pays us but with earth and dust;
>
> Who, in the dark and silent grave,
>
> When we have wandered all our ways,
>
> Shuts up the story of our days;
>
> But from this earth, this grave, this dust,
>
> My God shall raise me up, I trust.

Because Christ lives, all who go down to the grave may do so with the same trust that God will one day raise them up again.

CHAPTER NINE:

THE POWER OF HIS RESURRECTION

> *"I consider everything a loss compared with the surpassing greatness of knowing Christ ... and the power of his resurrection" (Ph 3:8-10)*

Somewhere years ago I read this story-

At the time of the Crimean War, Britain and France had an ally in their struggle against Russia, whose name was Samuel Schamyl (1797-1871). He was leader of the tribes of the Caucasus in their thirty years' struggle against the Csar. But victory depended upon making his people strong and welding them into a powerful nation.

To help achieve those goals he determined to remove corruption and bribery from high places. Accordingly, he passed a law that anyone found guilty of such practices would receive 100 lashes in the public square. It was a severe law, a harsh penalty, but the need was urgent.

Several people were caught and punished. Then tragedy struck at Schamyl. His own mother was found guilty of corrupt practice. He fasted for two days, but then with anguish passed sentence: **"One hundred lashes."** The people gathered. The old lady was bound to the stake. The lash fell once, twice, three times. She began to scream piteously. Schamyl could endure no more, and he roared, **"Stop the whip!"**

The people groaned; and as Schamyl's mother was being led away a sound of angry muttering began to rise, for they were fearful that anarchy would once again break loose upon them. But suddenly, every voice was hushed. Schamyl had torn the shirt off his own back. He stepped up to the stake. He wrapped his arms around it. He demanded that the usual chains be fastened on him.

Then he ordered the flogger to lay upon him with all strength the remaining ninety-seven lashes.

Why did he do it?

I suppose because he loved his mother, and because the law had to be upheld; but mostly because he knew that his mother would perish under the lash, while he was able to bear it and live again.

That is substitution. It is a picture of what Christ has wrought for us.

He loved you. He wished both to rescue you from certain and eternal death, yet also to maintain the law of God. So he took your place in death, exhausted the law's penalty, but then seized back his life so that he might carry his rescued friend with him into the heavenlies. There you are now seated, along with every Christian, a possessor of every spiritual blessing in Christ.

That is a song to tax the skills of a thousand angel choirs! No human words can ever hope to encompass such a sublime anthem! Yet we must try to do so in the next few pages, as we explore the treasures unlocked for us by Jesus' stunning victory over death.

Here then are -

(I) THE EFFECTS OF CHRIST'S RESURRECTION

(A) IT PROVED JESUS IS THE SON OF GOD

Paul wrote his first letter to the Thessalonians barely 20 years after the execution of Jesus. In that letter he boldly associates Jesus with God the Father, on equal terms (1:1). How could he do this? How could that strict Pharisee, a Jew in whose blood monotheism was a molten passion, dare to exalt a condemned malefactor to the right hand of God?

Only the resurrection could have achieved such an astonishing change in such a man as Paul.

He profoundly believed that God had raised Jesus of Nazareth from the dead in order to establish his divine identity. No wonder Paul was constrained to say,

> *"Jesus Christ our Lord was designated Son of God in power according to the Spirit of holiness by his resurrection from the dead" (Ro 1:4).*

Other prophets in earlier times had worked miracles equal to many of those wrought by Jesus himself during the years of his public ministry. But nothing like the resurrection had ever occurred before. The credentials of no other servant of God had ever been given such a stupendous attestation. The resurrection made it impossible to doubt that every one of the amazing claims Jesus had made about himself were absolutely true. He is indeed the Son of God, fully one with the Father in prestige and power.

(B) IT CONFIRMED THE MESSIAHSHIP OF CHRIST

Jesus had intimated that he was the promised Messiah; but whatever proofs may have been offered during his life to support this claim would seem, even to sympathetic friends, to have been nullified by his death. As for his enemies, they were certain that the cross confirmed their assessment of him as a blasphemer. Had not God rejected him - and in the most accursed manner? For the scripture itself says,

> *"a hanged man is accursed by God" (De 21:22-23).*

The cross, to a Jew, was a special sign of the blasphemer -

> *"He that blasphemeth God let him be stoned, and let him hang upon a tree all that day, and then let him be buried in an ignominious and obscure manner" (Josephus 4:8 (6)).*

So Jesus' enemies had no doubt that God himself had endorsed their opinion of him, and that his execution was actually an act of furious divine judgment. They were mightily pleased when they went to Pilate to request a guard of soldiers to prevent "that impostor" from fabricating a "resurrection" (Mt 27:62-66).

Imagine, then, their chagrin, when only a few weeks later the Christians began hurling the cross back into their teeth, and turning that emblem of shame into an insignia of the Messiah!

> *"The God of our fathers raised Jesus, whom you killed by hanging him on a tree. God exalted him at his right hand as Leader and Saviour, to give repentance to Israel and forgiveness of sins" (Ac 5:30-31; also 2:35; 10:39-40).*

The sheer daring of such a claim staggered the Jews; and the accusation it contained that they had murdered their own Messiah provoked them to terrible fury:

> *"When they heard these things they were enraged, and they ground their teeth against (them) (Ac 7:54).*

But nothing could staunch the revolutionary ideas that were born in the disciples after they had seen the risen Christ. Scriptures that for generations had been thought to proclaim only despicable guilt, were now seen to be the brightest nuggets of God. Thus was Paul able to flout every conventional interpretation:

> *"Christ redeemed us from the curse of the law, having become a curse for us - for it is written, 'Cursed is every one who hangs on a tree' " (Ga 3:13).*

But the word "cross" was so ugly to Jewish ears (far worse than "gibbet" sounds to us), and the idea of a crucified Messiah so repulsive to people who had expected a brilliant military leader, that not even the empty tomb could remove the scandal of the gospel (1 Co 1:23; stumbling block in Greek is *skandalon*). Thus they unwittingly, and blindly, continued to fulfil the prophecy:

> *"We steemed him stricken, smitten by God, and afflicted" (Is 53:4).*

According to Barnes, across the centuries a common Jewish epithet for Christ has been *tolvi* - "the man that was hanged"; and

Christians they have called *abdai tolvi* - "servants of the man that was hanged". But what they reckon for our shame we make our highest boast. It is our joy to be reckoned followers of the Crucified One, for by his resurrection the cross has been turned into the most exalted badge in the universe! We wear it with utmost pride. It marks our Leader, our Saviour, our Messiah.

(C) IT INAUGURATED JESUS' HEAVENLY MINISTRY

We rest upon the revelation of scripture that Christ has been lifted up to God's right hand, and that he is seated on heaven's loftiest throne. From there he exercises for ever his High Priestly ministry. But the ascension and exaltation of Christ (Ph 2:9-11; Mt 28:18) stand upon his resurrection. He was **raised** so that he might **reign** - except that he reigns now with a dual identity, Son of God, **and** Son of Man; whereas he reigned before only as Son of God.

It was his human identity that made the resurrection necessary.

As **Son of God**, he could have resumed his heavenly position any time he chose to do so; but he would then have reigned alone, without the "many sons" he desired to "bring to glory" (He 2:10). So he could not return to his Father as Son of God alone. A way had to be found, when he ascended back into heaven, for his human nature to remain allied with his divine nature.

That way was the resurrection.

Without the resurrection he might simply have continued reigning as the eternal Logos, in the form he had with the Father from the beginning; but his human flesh and nature would then have remained imprisoned for ever in hades, and all hope of salvation would have been lost to us.

But now we are sure of entering the holiest ourselves, and of being **"presented faultless before the Father"**, because Christ, bearing our likeness, has already gone before us. The ancient stricture, "no man can see God, and live" (Ex 33:20), is nullified, for the Man, Jesus of Nazareth, now sits at God's right hand!

Thus it is said that "it was <u>necessary</u> that Christ should suffer these things and enter into his glory" (Lu 24:26); and, "what God promised to the fathers, this he fulfilled to us their children <u>by raising Jesus</u>" (Ac 13:33).

(D) IT PROCLAIMED JESUS JUDGE OF ALL NATIONS

> "Of death and judgment, heaven and hell,
> Who oft doth think, must needs die well!"
> - Sir Walter Raleigh

Judging by the calmness with which he faced his own execution[70], Sir Walter must have often thought about death, judgment, heaven, and hell. He certainly "died well", as befits a gentleman and a Christian.

Not that this is always so. As Bunyan so vividly portrayed in **Pilgrim's Progress**, in the hour of death, even good Christians may sometimes be overwhelmed by terrors, and may have to

---

[70] See the end of your previous lesson.

struggle against the seeming decay of their faith[71]. But in general it is true. Those who before death have opened their minds to a vision of what lies beyond the veil, and who have taken refuge in Christ, can face death with equanimity.

---

[71] Bunyan describes Christian and Hopeful, at the end of their pilgrimage, coming to the river (death) they had to cross before they could enter the Celestial City -

"Now I further saw, that between them and the gate was a river but there was no bridge to go over; and the river was very deep. At the sight, therefore, of this river, the pilgrims were much stunned; but the men that went with them said, You must go through, or you cannot come at the gate.

"The Pilgrims ... asked the men if the waters were all of the same depth? They said, no; yet they could not help them in that case; for, they said, you shall find it deeper or shallower, as you believe in the King of the place.

"Then they addressed themselves to the water, and entering, Christian began to sink; and crying out to his good friend Hopeful, he said, 'I sink in deep waters; the billows go over my head; all thy waves go over me. Selah.'

"Then said the other, Be of good cheer, my brother; I feel the bottom, and it is good. Then said Christian, Ah! my friend, 'the sorrow of death hath compassed me about;'

I shall not see the land that floweth with milk and honey. And with that a great darkness and horror fell upon Christian, so that he could not see before him. Also here he in great measure lost his senses, so that he could neither remember nor orderly talk of any of those sweet refreshments that he had met with in the way of his pilgrimage. But all the words that he spoke still tended to discover that he had horror of mind, and heart fears that he should die in that river, and never obtain entrance in at the gate. Here also, as they who stood by perceived, he was much in troublesome thoughts of the sins that he had committed, both since and before he began to be a pilgrim. It was also observed that he was troubled with apparitions of hobgoblins and evil spirits; for ever and anon he would intimate so much by words ... "

Bunyan tells how Hopeful encouraged Christian, until he broke through all his fears, and the two pilgrims finally made their way across the river. Then follows a stirring and joyous description of their entrance into the golden City. It is altogether a marvellous scene.

Raleigh's couplet presupposes that those who have properly thought about death, will also have thought about the judgment that must follow (He 9:27), and that they have prepared themselves for both events. Whether he had truly done so himself, only the day of judgment itself will reveal. But we can at least be sure that day is inevitable, and if any would like to doubt it then their doubts have been turned into folly by the resurrection of Christ -

> *"God raised Christ on the third day ... and commanded us to preach to the people and to testify that he is the one ordained by God to be judge of the living and the dead ... God has fixed a day on which he will judge the world in righteousness by the man whom he has appointed, and of this he has given assurance to all men by raising him from the dead" (Ac 10:39-43; 17:31).*

If Christ did not rise, then we may as well eat, drink and be merry, for tomorrow we die, and there is no escape from the grave nor any coming wrath to fear. But if Christ **is** risen, then the day of judgment is certain, and we had better **prepare to meet our God** (Am 4:12; He 4:13).

(E) IT WAS THE BEGINNING OF THE NEW CREATION

Scripture describes Jesus as the **"last Adam"**, the first-born of a new race (1 Co 15:45,47; Cl 1:15,18; He 1:5-6). This new race is not headed by a man, like the first Adam, who could die, but by God's new Man, begotten from the dead, who cannot fail.

Notice also, he is called, not the "second" Adam (as though there might be a third, or fourth) but the "last" Adam. There will never be another, for there will never be need of another. This Man succeeded in all he had come to do. He perfectly obeyed the Father.

And just as the first Adam was called up from the dust of the earth by the word of God, so this last Adam was called out of the grave by that same word. Thus his righteousness was confirmed, and he was designated by God the beginning of the new creation, composed of redeemed men and women, whose own eternal righteousness is secured in Christ.

The sons of the old Adam were inextricably bound to their father's sin; the members of the new family are indissolubly united with their Founder's holiness (Ro 5:12-19).

How do we become part of the new family of God?

Simply by speaking the word of faith that brings us into mystical union with Christ - see Ga 2:20; Cl 1:26-27.

But none of this would have been possible without the resurrection.

Christ can be called the "last Adam" only because he was raised in the flesh, and ascended bodily into heaven, thus becoming the first of the new race to enter the holiest. The old Adam was the first man to stand in Eden. The last Adam was the first of the new creation to stand in Paradise (Lu 23:43).

(F) IT CHANGED THE APPEARANCE OF DEATH

How stunningly the resurrection of Christ changed the face of death! It has provided us with -

(1) A New Aspect On The Death Of Jesus

The resurrection compelled everyone who saw the empty tomb to look at the death of Jesus in a new light. Instead of speaking about that horrible hour in dolorous tones, they could now exult -

> *"It is Christ Jesus who died, yes, but who was raised from the dead, who is at the right hand of God, and who intercedes for us!" (Ro 8:34).*

As a result, the cross, instead of being an emblem of poverty, of failure, has become for Christians a prnmise of surpassing wealth and unfailing triumph -

> *"Since God did not spare his own Son, but gave him up for us all, will he not also freely give us all things with him?" (vs 32).*

How could it be otherwise? Alongside the gift of Calvary every other boon God could bestow pales into insignificance. If the Father was willing to sacrifice his only Son, it cannot be imagined that he will now withhold those lesser gifts we might desire from him!

> Christ was not spared -
>
> he was spared no sin
>
> > - so that we should lack no righteousness.
>
> he was spared no disease
>
> > - so that we should lack no healing.
>
> he was spared no poverty
>
> > - so that we should lack no wealth.
>
> he was spared no defeat
>
> > - so that we should lack no victory.

He was **denied** everything, so that we might **gain** everything. No **sorrow** was withheld from him, so that no **blessing** might be withheld from us.

The cross marks for us the extent of God's willingness to give us "all things" - all that we need for righteousness, health, prosperity, success, strength - in time and in eternity. There is a promise to stir the most sluggardly faith! Who can contemplate the cross, measuring the depth of Christ's loss and the height of the Father's gift, and not shout, **"I believe that God, who spared Christ nothing, will now deny me nothing!"**

But notice, this good promise, that God freely gives us **"all things"**, cannot be had independently of Christ. Paul is careful to say that God gives "all things <u>with</u> him (Christ)". God's gifts are bounded by Christ. There are both riches and restraint in those words:

- ➤ riches, because Christ himself is the greatest gift, in whom every lesser gift is contained. He who possesses Christ must already possess, with Christ, all else that the Father is able to give.
- ➤ restraint, because prayer will bring no gift outside of the parameters of Christ; that is, we cannot ask in Jesus' name for anything that is contrary to the character of Christ, nor opposed to his will.

So, while there is no theoretical limit to the gifts of righteousness, of health, of finance, of success, and so on, that the Father is able to give me with Christ, there may be practical limits imposed from time to time by his particular purpose for my life, or by my spiritual readiness to receive a particular gift.

Nonetheless, the problem with most Christians is not that they ask God for too much, but rather that they ask him for too little. We probably grieve the Father far more often by our small expectations, than we do by daring and grand requests. Surely the scripture challenges us to expand our faith to breathtaking limits when it says -

"Having given Christ to the cross, God is now willing freely to give us all things with Christ!"

There is a story told about Alexander the Great. He rewarded one of his soldiers by giving him an open order on the royal treasury. But when the soldier presented the order and demanded a huge sum of money, the treasurer refused to pay it. He was dismayed by the size of the soldier's demand. When Alexander heard about it, he was furious - with his treasurer. With burning indignation he rebuked the clerk: **"Do you not realise that my soldier magnifies the greatness of my kingdom by the greatness of his demand? Give him what he demands!"**

I often have the feeling that the Father is patiently waiting for me to do just that: **magnify the greatness of his kingdom by the greatness of my demands.**

It is sadly true: if the only measure people had of our God was the measure given him in our prayers, they would reckon him a small god indeed. They would never imagine he is the Lord of the whole earth, the possessor of the cattle on a thousand hills, and of the wealth in every mine (Ps 50:10-12)!

If a stranger heard you praying, how big would he reckon your God to be? Remember, his only measure is your prayer. Would he reckon that God is wealthy and mighty, or helpless and impoverished?

There is nothing like a clear sight of the empty tomb to enlarge faith. If God could give Christ to death, and then raise him again, there is nothing he cannot do. Our praying should all be done in the power of the resurrection. We should tolerate no boundary around our expectations smaller than the boundary drawn by the resurrection. The resurrection has created a new dimension to human understanding of the power of God. The resurrection has transformed Christ from just one more religious martyr into the Prince of Life (Ac 3:15; 5:31).

(2) A New Aspect On Our Death

Easter Sunday is an unchanging demonstration that death should never again terrify man. Christ has broken the power of death, and now guarantees eternal life to all who place their trust in him - Jn 14:19; 1 Co 15:54-57; He 2:15. Because Jesus is alive, we can live with joy, declaring ourselves ready to die; for we know that death cannot overcome the life of Christ that is in us.

In fact, only those who are ready to die are ready to live - for what kind of life can a person have who is shadowed by irrevocable death? And what is there, save an experience of the resurrection life of Christ, that can fit a man or woman to face death, not with fatalism nor despair, but with gladness, like those who have found the secret entrance to a glorious palace? (Is 51:11; 33:17, 20-22).

(G) IT IS THE SURETY OF OUR SALVATION

Against those who argue that the bodily resurrection of Jesus is not an essential part of Christian belief, we place Paul's emphatic claims that our salvation is made or unmade by the question of the empty tomb. If the record is true that an angel said, **"He is not here, for he is risen,"** then we who believe are the happiest people on earth. But if the record is false, then we are of all people the most wretched - 1 Co 15:17-19; see also Ac 17:31; 1 Co 6:14; Ga 1:1; Ep 1:19-20; Ga 2:12; etc. The empty tomb is implicit in all of those references, and it becomes the fulcrum of Christian hope.

Christ himself, we are told, appeared to eleven of the disciples and **"upbraided them for their unbelief and hardness of heart, because they had not believed those who saw him after he had risen"** (Mk 16:14). There is simply no gospel without the empty tomb, and salvation belongs only to those who believe that God raised Jesus from the dead (Ro 10:9-10).

But why is it so important to believe wholeheartedly that Jesus walked out of the tomb on that first Easter morning?

Simply because there is no other way to experience personally the resurrection life of Christ.

We are called not just to believe the **doctrine** of the resurrection, but to **experience its power**!

The empty tomb is a striking demonstration of the mighty ability of God that is now at work in those who believe. If Christ is really alive, then we can do no other than affirm with Paul -

> *"I am willing to suffer the loss of everything, and to reckon the whole world a dung heap, if only I may gain Christ and* the power of his resurrection*!" (Ph 3:8-10).*

What can possibly compare with this knowledge? What can be more valuable than this power? What can be more desirable than this resurrection life?

Observe two important things -

(1) This power is freely available

The proper state for every Christian is to live with a continuing experience of the resurrection life of Christ - 2 Co 13:3; Ep 1:19-20; Ro 8:11; 1 Pe 1:5-7.

Yet not all Christians live in that state; because, while the power of Christ's resurrection is in one sense freely available, there is another sense in which

(2) There is a price to pay for this power

> *"I am willing to suffer the loss of everything, and to reckon the whole world a dung heap!*

Perhaps you think such an astonishing renunciation is too extreme? Perhaps Paul is exaggerating? Surely discovery of the resurrection cannot be worth the loss of **"all things"**? Yes, it is. Because the real **power** of the resurrection cannot be known apart from Jesus himself. You see, people can accept the resurrection as an historical fact without ever discovering its **power** because that discovery depends on knowledge of Christ -

> *"That I may know him and the power of his resurrection" (Ph 3:10).*

This "knowing" is more than just a doctrinal appreciation of Christ; rather, it is knowing him warmly, vitally, personally - more really than the disciples knew him in Palestine (cp. 2 Co 5:16). This kind of knowledge, says Paul, is costly. It comes neither cheaply nor easily. In fact, Paul suggests there are times when it might cost a man all that he has to so know Christ; he might have to renounce everything he possesses, to treat it like rubbish, just to gain this knowledge.

When you think about it, that is not surprising, for it is always costly to know someone. To gain any true friend you have to surrender some of your own wants and ways. Any happy marriage is a demonstration of this. What couple can build an intimate and fulfilling relationship without continual surrender to each other of many personal possessions and prerogatives?

The cost involved in discovering another person is an inescapable principle of human relationships. It is coupled with a corollary principle: **the more noble the character of the person you desire to know, the greater the cost is likely to be.** Can a cheat and liar keep to his ways yet hope to befriend a virtuous man? Can a man who washes infrequently live pleasantly with a man who is scrupulously clean? Will a well-dressed man walk contentedly with a person who delights only in rags? How long will deep friendship endure between one who is well-spoken and another whose tongue is perpetually foul? Will love long survive between one who is peaceable and another who is always quarrelsome?

If I do want to know a person of noble character then I must be willing to conform myself to that person. I cannot cling to rags, uncleanness, violence, and reasonably expect my friend to continue making me welcome, to seat me at his table, to converse with me as an equal, to make available to me all that is his.

Likewise, it is not possible really to know Christ without being willing to pay the price of conformity to his nature. In essence, that means placing greater value on **spiritual** things than on **material** things. So, later in the same chapter (Ph 3), Paul speaks with tears about some people in the church who had no hope of being the friends of Christ. On the contrary, they were his **enemies**, though they pretended to themselves that they were Christians -

> *"For many, of whom I have often told you and now tell you even with tears, live as enemies of the cross of Christ. Their end is destruction, their god is*

> *their belly, and they glory in their shame, with minds set on earthly things" (vs 18-19).*

There is a perfect description of how **not** to know Christ, and how never to discover the power of his resurrection!

By contrast, Paul then gives a picture of true Christians, and shows how we can tell whether we are walking properly in the way of the Lord - see vs 20-21.

> *(a) We live as the citizens of heaven*

> *"Our citizenship is in heaven."*

That saying had special meaning for the Christians at Philippi, for their city was a Roman colony. William Barclay writes -

> *"These Roman colonies were amazing places. Here and there at strategic military centres the Romans set down their colonies. They were not like modern colonies out in the unexplored wilds; they commanded great road centres, and passes across the hills, and routes by which the armies must march. In such places the Romans set down colonies, whose citizens were mostly soldiers who had served their time - twenty-one years - and who had been rewarded with full (Roman) citizenship.*

> *"Now the great characteristic of these Roman colonies was that, wherever they were, they remained fragments of Rome. No matter where they were, Roman dress was worn; Roman magistrates governed them; the Latin tongue was spoken; Roman justice was administered; Roman morals were observed. Even in the ends of the earth these colonies remained unshakeably and unalterably Roman.*

> *"So Paul says to the Philippians, 'Just as the Roman colonists never forget that they belong to*

> *Rome, you must never forget that you are citizens of heaven, and your conduct must match your citizenship[72]."*

Notice that two things were true of those ancient colonies -

    (i) The laws of Rome took precedence over the local laws.

Likewise, the laws of the kingdom of God must take precedence for us over every other rule or authority. We obey the word of God before we obey any other; we believe the word of God before we believe any other. That word governs our thought and our faith. We accept its testimony above that of any man, or devil, or even our own. We are resolved to say only what the word says, to bring all of our confession into harmony with the promises of God. We know that the laws of the kingdom have authority and power to supplant every other spiritual and natural law. In the unbreakable integrity of those laws we place full confidence, knowing that heaven may pass away, but the word of God endures for ever.

    (ii) The colonists were proud of the name "Roman", and proud to live, speak, and dress like Romans.

So it should be our joy to display at all times the marks of a Christian. One of the chief of these is -

    (b) We look for the Saviour

"We look for the Saviour, the Lord Jesus Christ."

Daily expecting the return of Christ is a mark of the true Christian. It is certainly **not** a characteristic of those who are "enemies" of the cross. For them no prospect could be less appealing; to them the thought of the second advent is repugnant, a source of fear.

But we who know Christ and the power of his resurrection cannot help but enter each day with the hope that **today Jesus may come.**

---

[72]   The Daily Study Bible, The Saint Andrew Press, Edinburgh; 1960; in loc.

We live on tip-toe, stretching with excitement toward the return of our Lord.

Notice the word **"look"**. It shows that the return of Christ will be **visible**. It will be **seen** by all men. There is no room in scripture for those spiritualising views that say the promises of Christ's return are fulfilled whenever a Christian dies. Death involves the believer going into heaven, with the Lord looking for the believer's coming; while scripture shows that Christ will come from heaven to us, and that we are on earth, looking for him.

Notice also the word **"Saviour"**. This word does not occur in the NT as often as might be expected, probably because it was commonly used in the Roman world to describe Caesar, who was called **"the saviour of mankind"**. The emperors took that title, and the populace was happy to acknowledge it, because the **Pax Romana** had spread peace throughout the empire for 200 years.

But now, writing to a Roman colony, Paul deliberately laid hold of the emperor's title and applied it to Christ. It was a bold stroke. And it declared Paul's belief that the Roman peace, imposed by the Caesars, cannot be compared with the **Pax Christus** that will follow the coming of the true Saviour of mankind - for he, too, will come to a warring and desperate world, just in time to preserve the human race from terrible self-destruction (Mt 24, Mk 13, Lu 12).

(c) We long for the resurrection

"He will change our lowly bodies to be like his glorious body."

The language here leaves no doubt that our **present** bodies will be raised and transformed in the day of general resurrection. This answers those who say (i) that there will be no actual resurrection of the dead; (ii) that we shall not be **raised** out of the grave so much as **re-created** from the dust of God's memory of what we were - but that would be a replication, not a resurrection.

Paul is emphatic: "God will change my (present) lowly body." It is **this** body that will be sown in death; and it is **this** body that will be raised.

The body is described as **lowly**; which may be taken to mean -

      (i) Though the body sinks low in the grave, and becomes corrupted there, God is still able to raise it.

      (ii) Though the body may presently be laid physically low by disease, and morally low by sin, it will be raised by God holy and strong.

      (iii) Though the body has been made lowly and filled with humiliation by the Fall, in the hour of resurrection it will be restored to its original dominion and beauty.

In particular, our present **"lowly bodies"** will be **"changed to be like his glorious body"**. This cannot mean that we shall be identical to Christ in outward appearance, but rather that our resurrection bodies will take on the nature and character of Christ's body. That is, they will

- be given immortality

- become **"spiritual bodies"** in place of their present natural form

- assume a splendour above that of the angels (Ps 8:5, RSV)

- break free from the time and space limitations presently imposed on them.

We might well hasten toward such a goal!

    (d) We laugh at the doubters

"The question occurs, however, 'But how will this be possible?' What about those martyrs who were devoured by lions? What about those who were burned alive? Yes, what about millions of others, particles of whose dead and decaying bodies, through various stages of disintegration, finally enter into other living bodies? An answer that would be completely 'satisfying' to the mind of man - the mind darkened by sin! - is not available. One outstanding fact remains, however. That fact is the almighty power of One who could not be held even by death. Hence the apostle concludes this exalted paragraph by saying, 'Christ will do this by the exertion (or exercise) of that power which enables him to subject even all things to himself73.' "

(i) See the **simplicity** of the task

If Christ is able "even" to subdue all things beneath his will, how can it be supposed that raising the dead is beyond his ability? Not even "the totality of all the powers of the universe" can hope to thwart his will. Who then, or what, will be able to prevent him from gathering from the four corners of the earth his own elect, who fell asleep in Christ wanting and waiting for the resurrection?

Thus a mourner, standing at the grave of a beloved child, may say with calm beauty -

> But must we say she's dead? May't not be said
>
> That as a sundered clock is piecemeal laid,
>
> Not to be lost, but by the maker's hand
>
> Repolished, without error then to stand,
>
> Or as the Afric Niger stream enwombs
>
> Itself into the earth, and after comes
>
> (Having first made a natural bridge, to pass
>
> For many leagues) far greater than it was,
>
> May't not be said, that her grave shall restore

---

[73] William Hendriksen, New Testament Commentary, "Philippians"; Baker Book House, Grand Rapids, Michigan; 1974; in loc.

Her, greater, purer, firmer, than before[74]?

(ii) See the **magnitude** of the task

"By the power that enables him to bring everything under his control."

Though raising the dead certainly lies within the compass of divine ability, the resurrection remains nonetheless an act of omnipotent deity, a manifestation of the measureless force of God. The Greek phrase is strong. It couples two words that are the source of our words "energy" and "dynamic". It could be paraphrased, **"the energy of God's dynamic"**, where **dynamic** expresses God's awesome might, and **energy** expresses his power in action.

So here is all the energy of the Godhead, concentrated for a moment of time upon the single divine act of raising the dead. Under the impact of that colossal force, the dead will stir, and will be irresistibly called out of their graves, and raised up to meet their Lord.

---

[74] From John Donne's poem A Funeral Elegy. A. J. Smith mentions that "Donne follows the common opinion in the sixteenth century that the Niger flows eastward into the Nile, partly above ground and partly underground."

CHAPTER TEN:

LIVING VICTORIOUSLY

Have you ever wondered what is the one real key to Christian victory? Perhaps there is no single solution to every problem you will encounter. But Paul, in Ro 6:3-7, 11-13, certainly makes the death, burial, and resurrection of Christ a major element of a life of freedom and righteousness. Here is a powerful antidote to the problems that beset many Christians. Problems such as

> lack of sexual control
>
> unruly thoughts
>
> love of money
>
> uncontrollable anger
>
> jealous nature
>
> selfish spirit
>
> critical attitude
>
> pessimistic disposition
>
> addiction to some drug
>
> quarrelsome temperament

or such things as pride, anxiety, bad language, gossip, lying, gluttony, cruelty, laziness, and so on.

Paul's answer to such problems is to say that they are in fact **not** your problem. He describes them as **"works of the flesh"**; they belong to your old nature; they come from Adam, not from Christ. That old Adamic nature is your real problem, indeed, your only problem. Find a way to nullify that old nature, and all of its works will at once vanish also.

The issue comes down to this: who is going to prevail over you? **Adam**? Or **Christ**?

That at least has the merit of simplifying the problem. We no longer have to deal with a multitude of sins, one by one. We may instead concentrate our faith on this one matter of annihilating the old Adam.

How is that done?

(I) THREE RESULTS OF CHRIST'S RESURRECTION

At this point we are actually resuming the theme of the previous chapter: The effects of Christ's resurrection. We have so far seen seven of those effects; now we have three more, each related to some aspect of the victory created for us by the empty tomb. Thus we can say that the resurrection of Jesus is

(A) A KEY TO CHRISTIAN VICTORY

(1) Victory Does Not Come By Struggling, But By Believing

Satan's most successful ploy has been to get Christians to focus their attention on particular sins, instead of concentrating on Christ. Yet we should not devote our energy even to combating the old nature, but rather upon the task of clothing ourselves with the new nature God has provided for us in Christ.

Now that is a faith process, not an emotional one. We are asked to believe, not to weep, nor struggle, nor even pray.

How did Peter walk on water - by will-power, or by faith? How did Jesus ride an untamed colt - by brute strength, or by faith? How did Daniel remain in the lion's den unharmed - by physical agility, or by faith? Such examples could, of course, be multiplied. But always the same issue is prominent. The servants of God did their many exploits, not by exercising human ingenuity or muscle, but by faith (see He 11:1-40).

We too must get it fixed into our spirits that there is only one way for us to overcome the things that beset us, and that is the way of **faith**. Hence we are challenged to -

(2) Believe three things, just because God says they are true

(a) Believe you are DEAD with Christ

> "All of us who have been baptised into Christ Jesus were baptised into his death ... We have been united with him in a death like his ... We know that our old self was crucified with him ... We have died with Christ" (vs 3-6,8).

The point of this analogy is that a dead man cannot sin. He is beyond the power of temptation. All his passions, his desires, are cold: **"he who has died is freed from sin"** (vs 7).

If my "old self" was put to death with Christ, on the cross, then I have been freed from sin. This "death" is **potentially** true for each Christian, but it becomes true in practice only by reckoning it so by faith.

I may not **feel** that I am "dead". I may see evidence every day that my old self is very much alive. The works of Adam may be rampart in me. But I am still called by God to reckon myself dead to sin and alive to righteousness.

The question is, who am I going to believe: Adam, or Christ? Adam speaks to me through the sinful works of my old nature. I can listen to his voice, refuse to believe that I really did "die" with Christ, and so deprive myself of the only basis for victory provided by God. Or I can decline to recognise Adam's testimony, and set myself instead to hear the voice of Christ, who speaks through scripture. He tells me that I truly died with him, that my old self has been crucified, and that, as a dead man, I am freed from sin (from its guilt, and from its power).

Now if I determine to believe that word of Christ, no matter what my earthly senses may be telling me about my condition, then I have taken the first major step toward discovering the resurrection life of Christ. How can I experience resurrection unless I first die? So Paul rightly says -

> *"If we have been united with him in a death like his, we shall certainly be united with him in a resurrection like his!" (vs 5).*

Act now, in faith, to declare that your Adamic nature was crucified with Christ, and that it is now thoroughly dead. Do it, because God says so, regardless of what may be transpiring in your flesh.

> *(b) Believe that you are BURIED with Christ*
>
> *"We were buried with him by baptism" (vs 4).*

The second stage in the drama of redemption was burial. By faith we must see ourselves being taken with Christ into the grave. Wrapped around us are the graveclothes of the old nature. We are buried in anticipation of the resurrection, knowing that when we rise, the graveclothes will be left behind. We see them there still. The old nature and all its works, lying entombed. Death has overtaken it, and it has no power to rise again. If it should ever try to escape the grave, we bury it again by confessing the scripture: "My old nature was buried with Christ."

We inter the flesh deeply, refusing to reckon that it can escape.

It is a faith stance, based on the declaration of God who calls me to believe that my old self was surely buried with Christ.

> *I visualise it now, imprisoned forever in the uttermost depths (Mi 7:19-20).*

This idea is nicely illustrated by one of Grimm's fairy tales, **The Wilful Child** -

> *"Once upon a time there was a child who was wilful, and would not do what her mother wished. For this reason God had no pleasure in her, and let her become ill, and no doctor could do her any good, and in a short time she lay on her death-bed. When she had been lowered into her grave, and the*

> *earth was spread all over her, all at once her arm came out again, and stretched upwards, and when they had put it in and spread fresh earth over it, it was all to no purpose, for the arm always came out again. Then the mother herself was obliged to go to the grave, and strike the arm with a rod, and when she had done that, it was drawn in, and then at last her child had rest beneath the ground."*

Now that makes a graphic picture of your stubborn and wilful "old self". It has been buried with Christ, but keeps thrusting itself back up from the grave. It refuses to rest in peace. Nor is it any use to toil against it in the flesh, trying to bury it again beneath the fresh earth of your own efforts. It will remain too strong for even your sweatiest struggles. But a blow from the rod of faith will compel it to withdraw, and to submit quietly to death, and to keep its place in the grave!

> *(c) Believe that you are RAISED with Christ*

> *"So that as Christ was raised from the dead by the glory of the Father, we too might walk in newness of life ... united with him in a resurrection like his ... If we have died with Christ, we believe that we shall also live with him" (vs 4-5, & 8).*

Firm faith that I am **dead** with Christ, and **buried** with Christ, opens the way for me to believe also that I am now **risen** with Christ. This faith brings me to a tangible experience of the resurrection life of Christ, by which I can serve God in righteousness.

Notice that this life does not come to me as a weapon to use against sin, but as a source of strength to serve God. Sin is handled **passively**, by reckoning it dead and done away with; righteousness is handled **actively**, by an appropriation of the life of Christ that enables me to do the Father's will.

In the case of sin, there is nothing for me to do, except to believe that the work is done. In the case of righteousness, there is much for me to do, as I seize the ability God himself gives me through Christ, and then set myself to live for him. See vs 9-14.

Now none of this will happen unless you **believe** it.

Faith is the key!

Faith is the magic touch that places sin where it belongs; it unlocks the resources of the living Christ into your life; it is the only way you will ever overcome sin and serve God.

Some of the old fables catch this idea. The kiss of a gentle and lovely maid brings a handsome prince out of a monstrous beast, or a loathsome toad. Perhaps the fables were more concerned to show how true love can transform the ugliest person into someone beautiful (at least to the lover). But they serve also to illustrate my point: that the grace and glory of Christ lie in you **now**, waiting only to be released by the kiss of faith[75]!

(3) God's intention is that you should live victoriously

> *"Our old self was crucified with Christ so that the sinful body might be destroyed, and we might no longer be enslaved to sin ... So you must consider yourself dead to sin and alive to God in Christ Jesus ... Yield yourselves to God as men who have been brought from death to life, and your members to God as instruments of righteousness" (vs 6,11,13).*

You must will to have it so. Continuance of sin must be intolerable to any Christian who has come to resurrection life in Christ. It is impossible that such a Christian could be content for sin to maintain its domination.

So refuse to allow the old nature to rise up and haunt you from the grave. Even if defeat should overtake you, bury it again by joyful affirmation of all that you are in Christ.

---

[75] See the Addenda for two famous examples of the Fairytale Principle -

Allow nothing that belongs to your old self to deter you from declaring that you are, and always will be, dead with Christ, buried with Christ, and alive with Christ, with one heart only, to serve God in righteousness -

> *"For sin shall have no dominion over you, since you are not under law, but under grace" (vs 14).*

(B) THE SEAL OF GOD ON OUR JUSTIFICATION

> *"Christ was put to death (because of) our sins, and raised (because of) our justification" (Ro 4:25).*

That passage establishes an intimate link between four things: sin/death, and resurrection/justification. Without the death of Christ there would have been no atonement for our sin; but without the resurrection of Christ that atonement could never have been turned into our personal justification.

Elsewhere, scripture declares that we are actually justified by faith in the efficacy of the cross (Ro 5:9; etc); but we would never have arrived at this faith if Christ had not risen from the dead. As I have already suggested, it was the resurrection that turned an act of religious martyrdom into a supernatural atonement for the sin of all mankind.

The resurrection of Christ thus gains a double significance: it is evidential, and instrumental -

(C) IT IS EVIDENTIAL

It proves that the atonement was accepted by God; at the moment of his death, nothing was lacking of the righteousness Christ had come to fulfil. Thus the resurrection provided a testimonial of the sinlessness of Jesus, and it now gives us grounds upon which to believe in the value of the cross.

The Romans crucified thousands of Jewish men. Only one of them was raised from the dead by a prodigious act of divine power. His death was thus shown to be unique, and to have boundless value in the sight of God.

Yet that is only half the story. If the resurrection was only an event in history, if its value is nothing more than evidential, then Paul could not have written, **"Christ was raised because of our justification."**

Those words show that our justification does not depend exclusively on the cross (as is commonly thought), but there is also an indissoluble link between the **resurrection** and our justification. Suppose Christ had not risen. Not only would we have remained ignorant of the atoning value of the cross, but we would still not be justified even if we **did** somehow discover that Jesus had died for our sin. It is enough that the Sinless One should die. He must also rise from the dead.

There are those who hold that our justification **does** depend only on the cross, and that the resurrection is external to Calvary, having no direct influence on it. But that would make the resurrection nothing more than a prop to faith. It **is** that; but it is much more than that. For if the resurrection were only a prop to faith, then once faith was gained, belief in the resurrection would become unimportant. The same would be true if faith in the cross could be gained independently of the resurrection.

Some modern scholars argue in just that fashion: the resurrection story (they say) was constructed by the early church as a means of creating faith in Christ. The apostles wanted to show their intense belief that nothing could destroy the spirit of Jesus, that although his body may have been destroyed, Jesus himself was still very much alive. So they invented the story of the empty tomb. This device was necessary to help the people of those primitive times grasp the mystery of Christ. His survival beyond death had to be expressed in terms they could understand; that is, in terms of a bodily resurrection. But since belief in the living Christ is now firmly established, we can dispense with the resurrection story.

What a strange reversal! Once it was the cross that scandalised those who heard the gospel, and the resurrection was cited as God's vindication of Calvary. Now the resurrection itself has become the scandal. Modern man, it is said, cannot be asked to believe such a fantastic tale.

Such arguments deal unfairly with scripture. The resurrection cannot be relegated to mythical status; neither can it be limited to a certificate of divine approval upon the life and death of Jesus. If justice is going to be done to the witness of the apostles, then, while acknowledging the evidential value of the resurrection, we must also teach that -

(D) IT IS INSTRUMENTAL

Scripture insists that the resurrection effects a change in both Christ and man -

(1) In Christ

Christ arose from the grave invested for ever with the attributes of humanity, bearing for ever the marks of his death, presenting for ever to the Father the virtues of Calvary. Heaven and earth can never again be what they were before the day of his triumph. Eternal changes were wrought, beginning at the throne of God itself, and spreading out to the whole universe. These changes can be summarised as follows. The resurrection

- ➢ established Christ as the exalted Head of God's new creation, the last Adam, the progenitor of a new and irresistibly successful race, one over which neither sin nor death can ever again prevail.

- ➢ proclaimed Christ the only Redeemer of mankind, putting an end to any hope of obtaining righteousness by the works of the law, and marking him as the one Way, the absolute Truth, the perfect Life, the open Door, the inextinguishable Light.

- ➢ inaugurated the unshakeable kingdom of God on earth, in fulfilment of the prophets, thus beginning a program of divine activity among the nations that will find its climax in the return of Christ at the end of this present age.

- altered the nature of Christ's eternal sovereignty, for he reigns now not just as the divine Logos, infinitely distant from mankind, but as the peer of all men, who by sharing our human condition and triumphing over it, has vindicated the justice of God and fitted himself to be our king, not in tyranny, but in brotherhood.

- brought Christ into a new relationship with the whole creation; for having become part of the creation and making himself dependent on it for nourishment and physical life, he yet showed by his resurrection that the spiritual remains dominant over the natural, thus demolishing for ever the lie that flesh is stronger than spirit; he also established a basis for removal of the curse which came upon all animate things when sin began.

- prepared the way for Christ's return as Judge and King; for who can gainsay his right to judge the race that murdered him, nor successfully resist his strength to do so, nor oppose the coronation of him who by his conquest over death has won for himself more gloriously than any other man in history the crown of empire.

- delivered justly into his hands the kingdom of darkness; for he could have shattered that evil realm by sheer force; but then heaven would have seemed as tyrannous as hell; so it became the justice of God to defeat Satan, not by violence, but by virtue, which was consummated by Jesus' resurrection.

(2) In Man

The resurrection is the source of our faith in Christ - not simply because it is an effective witness of the true identity of Christ, but because as a direct result of the resurrection we are brought into union with Christ. Our salvation is not just a matter of belief in the value of Christ's death; rather, it depends upon us actually becoming united with Christ. It is not the death of Christ that saves us, nor any other fact **about** Christ, but rather Christ **himself**. We are redeemed in practice by **him**, not by any **work** that he did.

Admittedly, it is convenient to talk as though this work, or that, were the effective means of our redemption - to say that we are redeemed by the blood, or saved by the cross, and so on - but such talk can be misleading. It is more accurate to think of the works of Christ as providing the basis which enables him to act, lawfully and personally, to effect our salvation.

Salvation is a process of coming into union with a loving Saviour, and through that union gaining access to the merits of his sacrificial work. We cannot reach those merits apart from union with Christ himself, and we could not reach Christ apart from the resurrection. Our faith in the risen Christ brings us into

"such living union with him that his life becomes identified with ours and ours with his. Because of this identification, or incorporation, Christ's acts are repeated in us so that in his death we die to sin, **'crucified with Christ'** (Ga 2:20), and in his life we live to righteousness. But it is only by his resurrection that Christ can thus come into such living union with men as to effect their redemption" (J. M. Shaw)

The thing to understand here is that no human being could have been brought into direct union with the Logos alone. Between fallen man and the pre-existent Christ there was an impassable hiatus. But that vast chasm was crossed by the incarnation. Humanity was linked with deity. The way was opened for mankind to enter into a family bond with God.

But all would have been nullified if Christ's divine nature alone had survived the cross. Fortunately, this is not so. He arose bodily from the grave, so that now he is in heaven as the God-Man, and is able to apply to the church the benefits he gained for it at Calvary. We might say that Calvary **purchased** redemption, but the resurrection **provides** it.

Be careful, though, not to create an artificial division between the dying of Christ and his rising from the dead, as though these were two different works with different aims. The work of Christ is one. It has one goal: **the salvation of fallen man.** We are redeemed by the united act of Christ dying and rising. Both are inseparable parts of the one great work of salvation.

Thus salvation is not merely a thing of past accomplishment, a matter of historical belief, **but rather a continuous experience of the life that results from real union with the risen Christ.**

(E) IT DECLARES JESUS' VICTORY OVER SATAN AND HADES

Adequate comment on this theme has been given in other parts of the VCC, so it will be sufficient to remark here -

(1) Christ has conquered hades in both of its main aspects -

(a) he has destroyed its power to imprison the dead by breaking out of it himself (Ac 2:31) and claiming its keys (Re 1:18); and

(b) he has removed for ever the terrors of its place of punishment ("the lake of fire") from those who believe in him (Re 20:6,15).

(2) When Christ was raised from the dead, he was exalted above every power - Satan's included: see Ep 1:15-23; etc.

(II) OUR RESPONSE TO CHRIST'S RESURRECTION

If it is true that Christ is risen from the dead, then it becomes impossible not to proclaim that -

(A) THIS IS THE GREATEST EVENT IN HISTORY

It is our custom to divide time into the era prior to Christ's birth, and the era after his birth. While no Christian would deny the wonder of the incarnation, yet the fact remains that the birth of

Jesus would not have been noted if he had not risen from the dead some thirty-three years later. The manger depends for its beauty on the empty tomb. So it would have been closer to the gospel to have made the resurrection of Christ the end of the old era and the beginning of the new. Only two of the gospels tell the story of Jesus' birth, but all four evangelists tell the story of his resurrection!

(B) THIS IS THE GREATEST POWER YOU CAN EXPERIENCE

I have already suggested that you should be willing, if it were necessary, to pay anything, to lose everything, just to know Christ and the power of his resurrection. This is because there is no greater power, nor is there any other knowledge that can so transform your life.

Think what happens to the person who really **believes** that Christ is risen, who has met the power of his resurrection, and who is living daily in that power. That person will

(1) Never Again Be Afraid Of What Is Happening

The resurrection proves that God has invaded this planet in the person of Jesus Christ. We are not alone. The world is not just staggering along on a mindless, haphazard, crazy course to destruction. God has set a plan in motion that is advancing unhindered toward its goal. There is no power in heaven, on earth, or in hell, that can prevent his plan from being fulfilled.

How futile were their attempts to seal the tomb, and to prevent Christ from fulfilling his promise to rise again! How futile are their attempts to stop the outworking of God's purposes in our time!

The resurrection puts a different colour into every happening, it is the basis of our confidence that the Father is in control. Living in the power of his resurrection we lose all fear of what man or nations may do. We know that "our times are in his hands" (Ps 31:15). All is well!

(2) Never Again Feel Unimportant

Think what limitless value is placed on your life, and on you personally, that in order to preserve you, and to carry you into the heavenlies, Christ was willing to suffer, die, and be raised again from the dead. All of this he would have done if you had been the only righteous person upon the face of the earth. If no other child of Adam had sinned, except you, Christ would still have come, and found a way to offer you his death as an atonement for your sin, and to rise again so that in union with him you might regain all that your sin has stolen from you.

That gives you a value beyond anything in the universe, except Jesus himself. And whether you are one person, or many millions, that value is undiminished. No one who has felt the power of Christ's resurrection at work within them can ever again feel insignificant, worthless, as though, measured against the vast sweep of the universe, they are no more than a dry leaf tossing in the wind.

(3) Never Again Value The Material Above The Spiritual

Having stood in front of the empty tomb, having seen the great stone rolled back, having felt the trembling of the earth, having seen the apparently invincible grip of death cast aside as though it were the touch of a strengthless child - who could ever again think that the things of time are more desirable than the things of eternity? Who could ever again value earth more than heaven, the flesh more than the spirit, the treasures of men more than the treasures of God?

Believing that our bodies are one day to be raised, because Christ's body was raised, we suddenly see a new glory attached to our mortal frame. It is no longer a thing to be despised. Nor can we keep a light view of sin; for sin can no longer be thought of as harming only a temporary flesh and bone dwelling - rather, sin attacks the body that is destined to be the eternal habitation of the human spirit (cp. 1 Co 6:13, 19).

If Abraham, who had so little upon which to build his faith, was yet willing to turn his back on the city of his fathers, and to look for the city of God (He 11:10), how much more should we, who have felt the power of Christ's resurrection! It is nothing for us to scorn those cities whose destiny is dust, and to reach for that city "which has foundations", for we know that the resurrection of Christ is an unstoppable vehicle, carrying us from destructible time into indestructible eternity!

(4) Never Again Believe That Death Is The End

How strong death has seemed to the passing generations! How final his dread sentence! How inescapable the grave! Yet suddenly he is made weak, his strength is dissipated. He no longer seems strong to me. Nor is he. For the resurrection-life of Christ that is in me is stronger than all death's power. Nothing can overwhelm it. Not even the complete decay of my mortal frame can disturb that power of life. It works in me now, and will never cease to work.

As long as Christ reigns, I reign. As long as he sits at the Father's right hand, I am blessed with every spiritual blessing in the heavenlies.

For those who believe, death is no end, but rather a joyous beginning. The grave is not a prison, but rather an open door to paradise. The cemetery is no longer a place of chilly dread, but the site of the most stupendous miracle the world will ever see: the miracle of the opening graves and the rising dead that will occur when the risen Christ returns in his glory.

Even so, come Lord Jesus!

ADENDUM:

Examples of the "Fairytale Principle"

I. Beauty and the Beast

(The maiden had returned to the Beast, only to find him lying apparently dead, clutching a rose that he associated with her) -

"She was too late. Her eyes brimmed with shame and pity. She put her slender arms about his shaggy neck and embraced him tenderly, a hot tear falling on his death-cold head. No sooner had she kissed him than lightning flashed on every side and a stone thunder-arrow struck the grassy mound. The girl fell senseless to the ground. When she awoke she found herself in a hall of white marble, sitting on a golden throne beside a young, handsome prince ... A grand wedding was held amid great rejoicing. And their happiness, being built on goodness, was complete."

(From **McDonald Fairy Tales**, as told by James Riordan; McDonald Educational Ltd., London, UK.; 1979.)

II. The Frog Prince

(A great ugly frog had rescued a golden ball that the princess had carelessly tossed into a well. As a reward, the frog demanded permission to eat at her table and sleep in her bed. With much reluctance and loathing the princess agreed. After a terrible night, the frog promised never again to torment the princess if she would but kiss him on the mouth.)

"The princess shut her eyes as tight as could be and kissed the frog. She had dreaded the touch of his mouth, but to her great surprise she found herself being delightfully kissed by warm, enthusiastic lips. She opened her eyes - and found herself in the arms of a tall, dark, handsome young man. 'Princess,' he explained, 'my name is Prince Conrad of Ruraliese. When I was christened, my parents forgot to invite my fairy godmother, but she turned up in a vile temper and changed me into a frog. Then she told me that I would remain a frog until a royal princess let me sit at her table, and share her meals, and afterwards allowed me to sleep on her pillow. And if she kissed me full on the mouth,' Conrad added, 'the spell would be broken and I would become my true self again.' "

(So they fell deliriously in love, married, and lived happily ever after.)

(From **The Full Colour Fairytale Book**; ed. R. C. Scriven; Derrydale Books, New York, USA.)

However, that version of **The Frog Prince** bears scant resemblance to the original fairy tale, and you may be interested in the following curious account. When I was writing this section of the lesson, I wanted to go back to the original legend of the frog who became a prince when a fair maiden kissed him. But after scouring various libraries, I was driven to conclude that there is no such ancient story! The nearest I could find was a fable in the Brothers Grimm collection, which is called **The Frog King**, or **Iron Heinrich**.

The surprising thing in that story is that the princess does not **kiss** the frog. On the contrary, her behaviour throughout the tale is petulant and altogether disagreeable -

"So she picked up the frog with her two fingers, carried him upstairs, and set him down in a corner. Soon after she had got into bed, he came crawling over to her and said, 'I'm tired and want to sleep as much as you do. Lift me up, or I'll tell your father!' This made the princess extremely angry, and after she picked him up, she threw him against the wall with all her might, crying, 'Now you can have your rest, you nasty frog!' However, when he fell to the ground, he was no longer a frog but a prince with kind and beautiful eyes"...

(From **The Complete Fairy Tales Of The Brothers Grimm**; tr. Jack Zipes; Bantam Books, New York; 1987; pg 5.)

In the original tale there is no mention of a kiss, nor of the name of the prince; both of those items seem to be later modifications of the Grimm version, although both are now well entrenched in popular fancy (which explains why **Conrad** was chosen as the name for an enchanted frog, the hero of a daily comic strip.) The prince remains unnamed in the original fable because its real hero is actually the prince's servant Heinrich (or Henry), who remained faithful while his master was under the spell. Thus the brothers Grimm entitled their version **Iron Heinrich** - commemorating the iron bands faithful Henry put around his chest to stop his heart from breaking. The tale ends with the bands cracking apart one by one under the pressure of Henry's joy.

One of our Australian VCC students was as convinced as I that there must **somewhere** be an original tale in which the princess **kisses** the frog. He too decided to research the matter. Here is part of a letter he wrote to me -

"(This problem) has got me intrigued! I put it to the infants department of our primary school, and they all "knew" of such a fairy story, most of them immediately suggesting it was a Hans Christian Anderson story. However, none of them could locate it, and **most** were thinking of Grimm's **Frog Prince**. I located **The Complete Works of Hans Christian Anderson**, but could not find (by title, index, or skim reading) any frog who was kissed. At my local municipal library were more than 200 volumes of fairy tales, but again no luck ... Out of curiosity, I read the 22 endings of the different accounts of **The Frog Prince** that I came across, and discovered three variations in the way he became a prince: (1) thrown against the wall; (2) changed overnight as he slept on her pillow; (3) changed as she pushed him out of the bed. None of them was with a kiss!" (**Tony Butz, Willoughby, NSW, Australia.**)

Plainly, modern re-tellers of the tale (like the one given above), are taking considerable liberty with the Grimm original when they make the princess **kiss** the frog!

However, Tony Butz did direct my attention to **The Classic Fairy Tales**, edited by Iona and Peter Opie. In their introduction to **The Frog Prince**, they discuss an ancient English tradition that probably has given rise to the popular notion of a kiss turning an enchanted frog into a prince. They write -

"**The Frog Prince** is another tale in which a handsome husband is won by a girl's acceptance of a creature that is at first repulsive to her. It is another tale, too, with a textual history that reveals the dilemma editors of English fairy tales sometimes have to face. Almost certainly the story of **The Frog Prince** has long been known in Britain, yet no satisfactory text has been preserved. When Sir Walter Scott saw the tale in the Grimm's (collection) he readily recalled from his childhood (he was born in 1771) a legend of a 'Prince Paddock' in which a princess was sent to fetch water in a sieve from the Well of the World's End, and that the feat was achieved by following the advice of a frog who obtained, in return, the princess's lightly-given promise to become its bride ... The idea that a kiss, or the marriage bed, could release a person from the curse of monstrousness, was one that thrilled readers in the Middle Ages ... Despite the fact that the story of **The Frog Prince** had, it seems, been common property in Scotland for three hundred years, also in Ireland and in Somerset ... the Grimm brothers in Hesse were the first to set down a complete telling of the tale." (Oxford University Press, UK.; 1974; pg 183,184.)

So it seems that the quest for an early version of the enchanted kiss turning a frog into a prince is doomed to fail. But the idea is firmly fixed in popular imagination. And the application of it in your lesson remains powerfully valid!

BIBLIOGRAPHY

Ante-Nicene Fathers; Vol 2; *Fathers of the Second Century*; Eerdmans Pub. Co., Michigan, 1979 reprint.

Athenian Popular Religion; by Jon D. Mikalson; University of North Carolina Press; 1983.

Authority and Authenticity of the Bible, The; Ken Chant; Vision Publishing, Australia.

Believer's Bible Commentary; William Macdonald; Thomas Nelson Publishers; 1989.

Bible Background Commentary; Intervarsity Press, Nottingham, UK. 1993.

Bible Knowledge Commentary, The; by John Walvoord and Roy Zuck; Cook Communications, Colorado Springs, Colorado, 1989.

Calvin's Commentaries; John Calvin (1509-1564).

City of God; tr. by Henry Bettenson; ed. by David Knowles; Penguin Books, London, 1972.

College Press NIV Commentary, The; Joplin, Missouri; 1996.

Commentary on Ephesians, A; Charles Hodge (1797-1878).

Commentary on the Bible; Adam Clarke (1715-1832).

Commentary On The Old And New Testaments, A; John Trapp (1601-1669).

Commentary on the Old and New Testaments, A; Robert Jamieson, A. R. Fausset, David Brown; 1871.

Daily Study Bible, The; The Saint Andrew Press; Edinburgh, 1960.

Emmanuel; Ken Chant; Vision Publishing; Australia.

Explanatory Notes on the Whole Bible; John Wesley (1703-1791).

Exposition of the Entire Bible; John Gill (1690-1771).

Expositor's Bible Commentary, The; ed. Frank E. Gaebelein; Zondervan Publishers, Grand Rapids, Michigan.

Expository Commentary; H.A. Ironside (1876-1951).

Full Colour Fairytale Book, The; ed. R. C. Scriven; Derrydale Books, New York, USA.

Greek Myths, The; Vols 1 & 2; Penguin Books; UK, 1975.

Hastings Dictionary of the New Testament; W. S. Simpson; Vol 2; Baker Book House, Michigan, 1973 reprint.

Healing in the OT & Healing in the NT; Ken Chant; Vision Publishing; Australia.

Hinduism, by Louis Renou; pub. by George Raziller; New York, 1962.

History of the Jewish Wars; Josephus.

Holman New Testament Commentary; ed. Max Anders; B & H Publishing Group, Nashville, Tennessee, 2004.

Honest to God; John Robinson; 1963.

I Believe in The Resurrection; G. E. Ladd; Hodder & Stoughton, 1975.

Interpreter's Bible, The; Abingdon Press, New York, 1952.

IVP New Testament Commentary Series, The; Intervarsity Press; Nottingham, UK.

Jewish New Testament Commentary; David H. Stern; Jewish New Testament Publications, Inc., Clarksville, Maryland, 1982.

Koran, The; tr. N.J.Dawood, Penguin Classics, 1980.

Matthew Henry's Commentary; Marshall, Morgan, and Scott, London, 1953.

Matthew Poole's Commentary; 1685.

Nelson's New Illustrated Bible Commentary; Thomas Nelson Inc., New York, 1999.

New International Commentary on the New Testament, The; Eerdmans Publishing Co. Michigan, 1977.

New Testament Commentary; Baker's Publishing House, Grand Rapids, Michigan, 1987.

New Testament Commentary; William Hendriksen, *Philippians*; Baker Book House, Grand Rapids, Michigan, 1974.

New Testament Word Studies; Kregel Publications; Grand Rapids, Michigan, 1971.

New Testament Words; SCM Press Ltd. London, 1964.

Nicene and Post-Nicene Fathers, The; *First Series*, Vol 9; edited by Philip Schaff; Wm. B. Eerdmans Pub. Co, Michigan, reprint 1978.

Notes on the Bible; Albert Barnes (1798-1870).

Odyssey, The; Book 11; *The Book of the Dead*; tr by E.V. Rieu; Penguin Classics, 1958.

Pensees; *Thoughts;* Blaise Pascal; tr. John Warrington; Published by J. M. Dent & Sons Ltd. London, 1973.

People's New Testament Commentary, The; B. W. Johnson; Word Search Corporation; Nashville, Tennessee, 2010.

People's New Testament, The; by B. W. Johnson; 1891.

Pictorial Encyclopedia of the Bible; ed. M.C.Tenney; Art. *The Third Day*; Zondervan Publishing House, Michigan.

Pilgrim's Progress; John Bunyan; Tee Publishing; 2nd edition, 2009.

Poor Man's Commentary On The Whole Bible, The; Robert Hawker, 1850.

Preacher's Commentary, The; Word Inc., Nashville, Tennessee, 1992.

Preacher's Outline and Sermon Bible; Word Search Corporation, Nashville, Tennessee; 2010.

Pulpit Commentary, The; ed. Joseph S. Exell, Henry Donald Maurice Spence-Jones; 1881.

Vincent's Word Studies; Marvin R. Vincent; 1886.

When The Trumpet Sounds; Ken Chant; Vision Publishing, Australia.

Who Moved the Stone? Frank Morison; Faber & Faber Ltd. London, 1930

Why I Am Not A Christian; Bertrand Russell; Unwin Books; London, 1975.

Wiersbe's Expository Outlines; Warren W. Wiersbe; Publisher, David C. Cook, Colorado Springs, Colorado.

Word Pictures In The New Testament; A. T. Robertson; 1933.
World's Living Religions, The; Pan Books; London, UK. 1964.

www.ingramcontent.com/pod-product-compliance
Lightning Source LLC
Chambersburg PA
CBHW061302110426
42742CB00012BA/2028